Photorealistic Painting

By Daniel K. Tennant

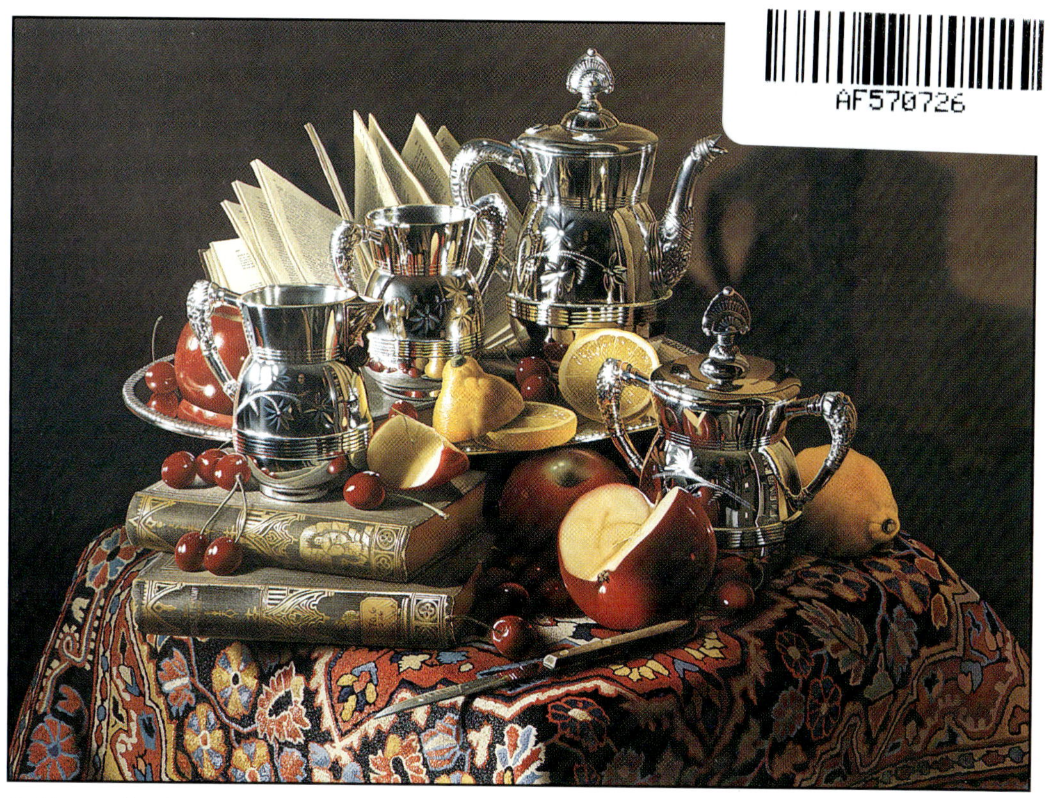

Heirlooms with Cherries (38-1/2" x 53") gouache on museum board, courtesy of Gallery Henoch, New York, NY

Walter Foster Publishing, Inc.
23062 La Cadena Drive, Laguna Hills, CA 92653

Contents

Introduction

Imagine yourself at an art show. A crowd is gathered around a certain painting—amazed that it looks so real. You overhear comments, such as "Wow! How did they do that?" and "It looks so real! I wish I could paint like that!"

There is a deep fascination with artwork that looks photographic. The aspiring painter often wonders how other artists are able to create works that are so persuasive. This book will show you step by step how these realistic effects are achieved. With practice, you will learn how to use an airbrush and traditional brushes to create paintings of striking realism.

One of the foundations of my technique is the use of gouache—or opaque watercolor. With gouache, light colors can be applied over a darker underpainting—a method not possible with some mediums, such as transparent watercolors.

The specific techniques and tools indicated herein are an important aspect of this book—and a prerequisite to success. Once you have mastered these techniques, there will be room for experimenting with other mediums, methods, and materials.

Without a camera you will be severely handicapped, because a photorealist painting is based on the use of photography as a sketching and reference tool. The artwork in this book was done from photographs. The necessity of working from photographs is obvious. For example, a still life setup of fresh fruit would not be fresh after two months. Photographs capture the moment and keep the subjects and lighting consistent.

The term "photorealism" was coined by J.W. Forger in 1961. It refers to a work so realistic that it looks like a photograph. Pure photorealists paint everything they see in a photograph—even lens flare or a crease. My work is photorealistic but modified to make a stronger painting. This book concentrates on the painting techniques of photorealism.

If you follow the instructions and try the demonstrations, you will be able to add new depth to your paintings and build on your newly acquired skills.

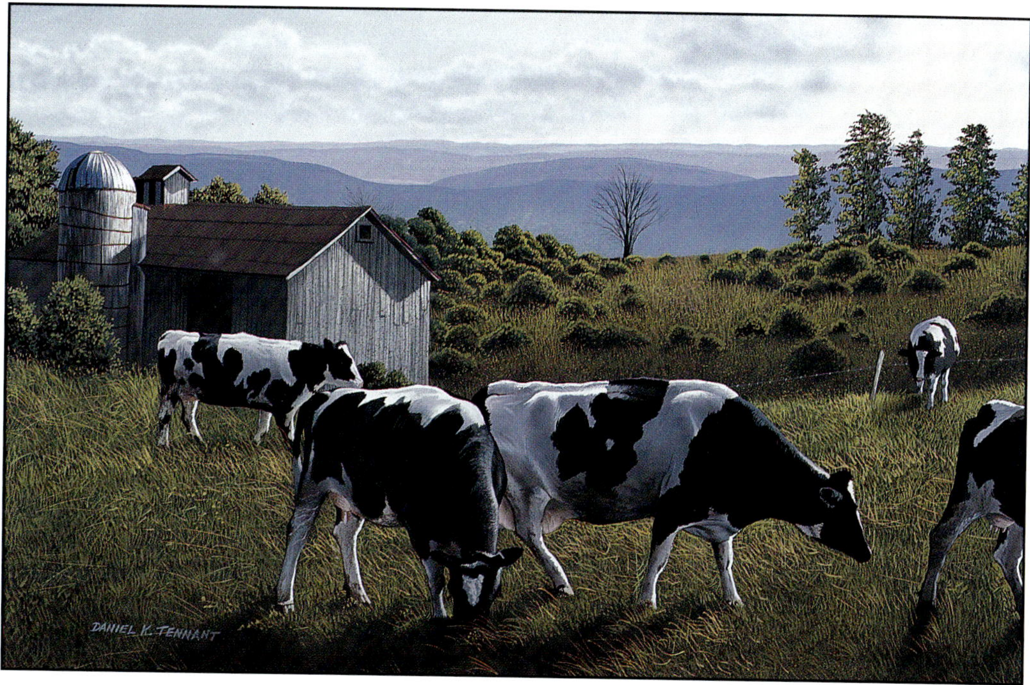

Country Evening **(24" x 30") gouache on illustration board, collection of Barry Parker**

Thoughts on Painting

Myths often surround the painting process—for example: painting is inspired; accomplished artists find painting easy and always succeed; painting is always fun; good artists only paint when they feel like it; and creating a good painting is unpredictable.

Let's dispel some of these myths. First, an artist does not have to be inspired to paint. A successful painting is predictable and logical, particularly in the photorealist style. I have often dragged myself into the studio, not feeling like doing much of anything. But then things start developing and I do feel inspired! Another common experience is "artist's slump." Sometimes, about halfway through a painting, I feel as if it is a loser and simply want to heave it—but I force myself to persevere. This is something all artists have to learn to overcome.

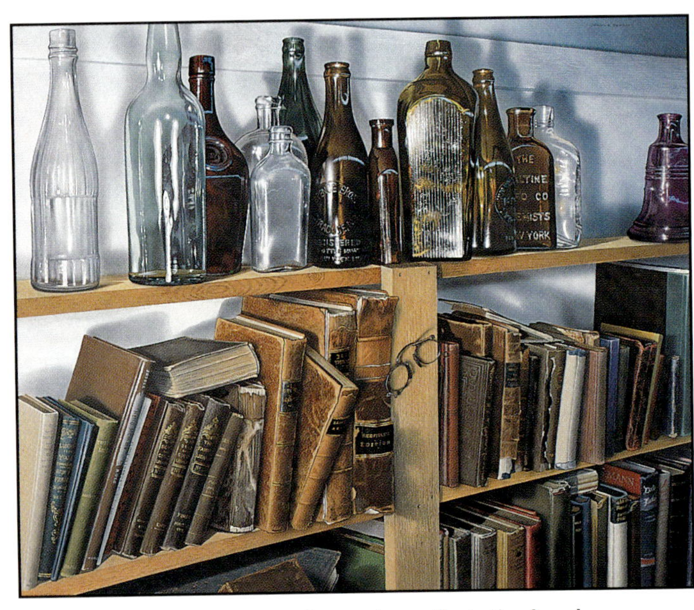

Still Life in a Bookshop **(40" x 50") gouache on illustration board, private collection**

Laying the Groundwork

When beginning a photorealist painting, keep the following tips in mind: (1) Resolve the drawing—composition, design, and balance—before you pick up a brush. There should be no guesswork; painting has enough challenges without having to worry about the fundamentals. (2) When you get frustrated, put the work away for a few days. Don't throw anything out when you're upset—it could be a mistake. (3) Use a mirror to look at your painting in progress. It gives a completely new view of your work. (4) When painting, find a comfortable place where you can make a mess. (5) Make color charts and keep them handy for mixing colors. These charts are important. One summer I made 1,200 color mixtures and placed them in a notebook for reference. (6) Finally, use this book as a reference for techniques and tips. The order in which you tackle a painting is crucial, so follow the suggestions throughout, and you will succeed.

Reference Materials

As mentioned previously, photos are used as references for photorealistic painting. There are many sources that will provide ideas: postcards, catalogs, travel brochures, family photos, magazine ads, art books, calendars, VCR still frames, art shows, posters, and your own imagination.

Invest in props that you will over and over, such as a drape, vase, bowl, or table. Also, buy a good 35mm camera and learn how to use it. Carry a small sketchbook and always be on the prowl for new material. When you see a potential subject, ask yourself how you would paint it. Try painting it in your head. Training your artist's eye is a lifelong habit that gets easier with practice.

Materials and Tools

For optimum results, always buy the best materials and tools you can afford. Inferior materials will make the project more difficult, which can be discouraging.

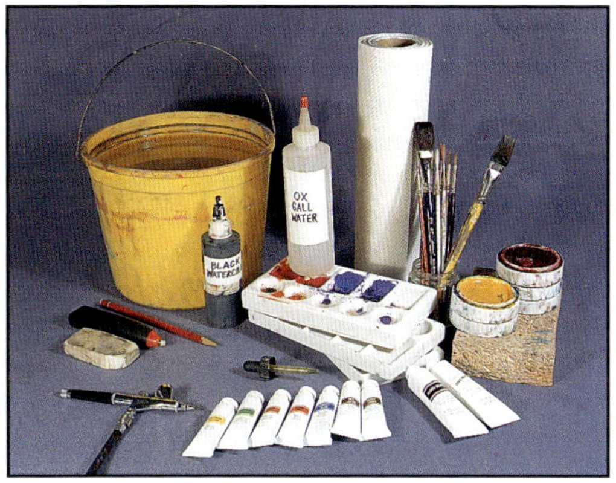

Gouache

Gouache is opaque watercolor (for more information, see page 12). For the best results, use high-quality, professional-grade paints, and select only those colors that are considered permanent. (Some pigments are fugitive, meaning that they fade when exposed to sunlight.) I recommend tubes over cakes because they are brighter, easier to mix large quantities of color, and have the best selection of color.

I use the following colors: alizarin crimson, burnt sienna, burnt umber, cadmium red light, cadmium red medium, cadmium yellow medium, cerulean blue, cobalt blue, ivory black, Naples yellow, permanent green light, titanium white, ultramarine blue, yellow ochre, and zinc white. Zinc white is the mixing white. Never use titanium white for mixing; it can cause colors to fade over time.

Bucket

A bucket of water is used for rinsing brushes between colors. Keeping your brushes clean will ensure bright colors and paintings.

Pencils

An HB pencil is good for preliminary drawings. HB lead is soft enough to leave a solid drawing, and gouache is not repelled when applied over it.

Erasers

Standard rubber or kneaded erasers are good for cleaning up drawings. A kneaded eraser is especially useful because the side can be used for erasing large areas, and it can be shaped to a point for erasing small areas.

Illustration Board

A hot-pressed (smooth) surface is recommended over a textured surface. It allows you to create your own textures. It also provides for the greatest amount of detail. The heavier the ply of the board, the better. (Four-ply is recommended.) Another option is museum board, which comes in an 8-ply weight. (Also see page 7.)

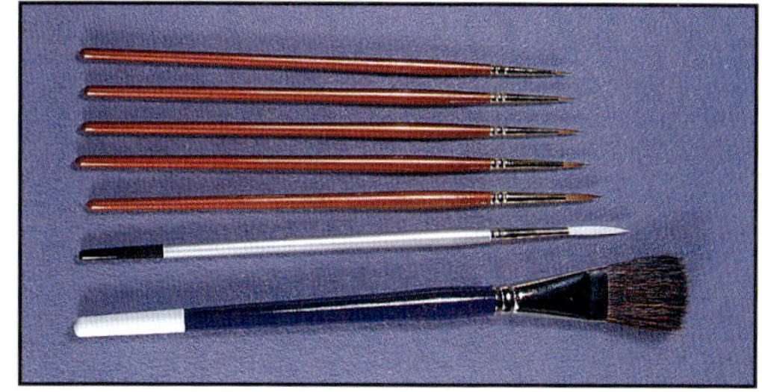

Brushes

I recommend using only red sable/synthetic-hair watercolor brushes and a large flat watercolor brush for large areas. One of each standard size—00, 0, 1, 2, 4, and 6—should suffice. (I use a #2 brush most often.) A long-haired rigger brush is good for making thin lines. The large flat watercolor brush is excellent for laying in backgrounds quickly and smoothly and covering large areas.

Good brushes are expensive, but if you wash them thoroughly after each painting session, they should last a long while. Rinse the brushes in cool or lukewarm (never hot) water, and lather them lightly with mild soap. Rinse them again, and then shape the hairs so they dry with a sharp point.

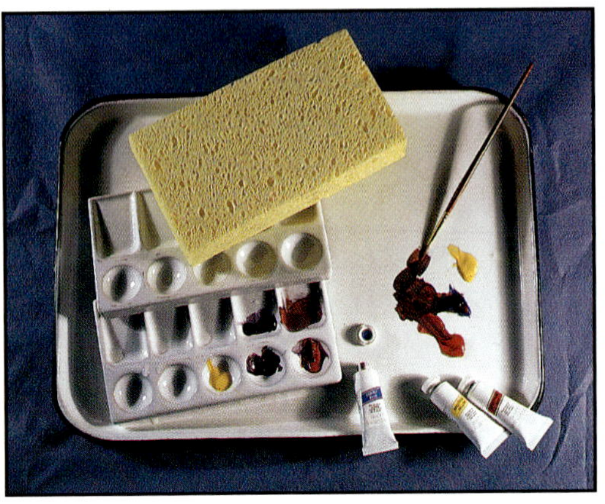

Palettes

There are many types of palettes available. My favorite is a china slant tile, which is made from baked ceramic and has 10 paint wells. It is portable, easy to clean, and has plenty of room for color mixing. A wet sponge laid over the entire tile will keep the paint wet for at least 24 hours. On extremely hot days, the sponge should be saturated with water. Other palette options include an enamel butcher's tray or a piece of plate glass or Plexiglas with toned paper placed underneath to help gauge colors.

Because gouache dries quickly, squeeze out only those colors that you will need in the next hour or so. (You can also drip some water from an eyedropper over the paints to keep them moist.) When painting one object at a time, squirt out the colors for just that object. I keep white and black at opposite ends of the palette so they don't get mixed into the colors. I often mix up tints and shades of colors as well. I might have light blue, blue, dark blue, black, and white on the palette when painting grapes. The fewer colors mixed, the brighter the paint will remain—and the painting as well.

Sponge

A large, synthetic sponge is moistened and then placed over the palette to keep the paints wet. This way, the paints should stay moist for at least a day.

Thinners

The only diluent needed for gouache is water. Tap water is fine if it is free from chemicals or other additives, such as fluoride. Some artists prefer to use distilled water purchased in gallon jugs. If desired, add one drop of ox gall to every two ounces of water. Ox gall is a pale, odorless wetting agent that causes the paint to dry more slowly, which allows for softer blending. With ox gall, the paint flows more evenly and does not puddle.

To ensure a more waterproof paint, you can thin gouache with water and acrylic medium. (Acrylic-gouache paints are also available. These paints are excellent but not as opaque as traditional gouache.) Thinning gouache with watercolor medium improves the flow of the colors and makes darks stay dark when dry. When gum arabic is added to water, it slows the drying time of gouache, maintains the darks, and increases the luminosity and brilliance of dried colors. Watercolor impasto gel enables you to apply gouache more thickly without cracking.

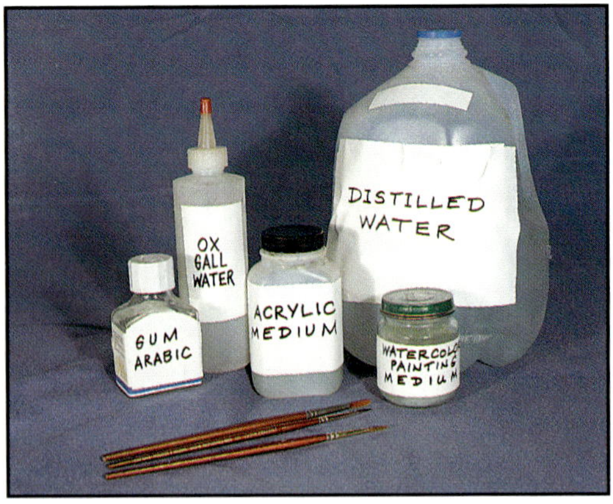

Airbrush

An airbrush uses compressed air to atomize paint and then applies it to the painting surface in a fine spray. Airbrushed paint has a soft, fuzzy appearance in comparison to the strokes of a paint brush. There are different types of airbrushes available. (See pages 16–17 for more information.)

Painting Surfaces

There are many surfaces from which to choose when painting with gouache; it will depend on the effect you want to achieve. An important point to remember is that gouache must be applied to a sturdy support. Paper that is too thin and flimsy will cause the paint to crack.

Gouache can be painted on gesso panel if traditional gesso is used. (I suggest staying away from acrylic gesso.) Illustration boards, museum mounting boards, and heavy drawing or watercolor papers (140-pound or heavier) are highly recommended. The most popular surface is hot-pressed, which is smooth. You can also buy cold-pressed (light tooth) or rough (heavy tooth) surfaces. Hot-pressed surfaces let you create your own textures, whereas textured surfaces already dictate to some degree the look of your painting. For highly realistic paintings, the hot-pressed surface is superior.

Gouache has strong covering ability. By painting on toned surfaces, some artists let small areas of the toned support show through to create an overall color harmony. Toulouse-Lautrec often used this effect with his beautiful gouache paintings of Parisian life in the late 1800s.

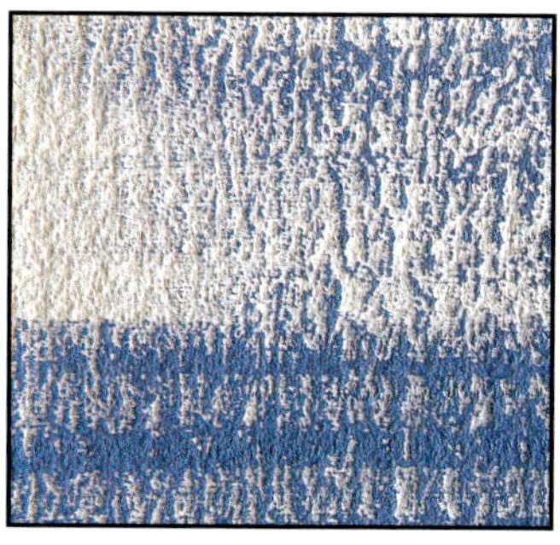

Rough watercolor paper tends to exaggerate airbrush spray.

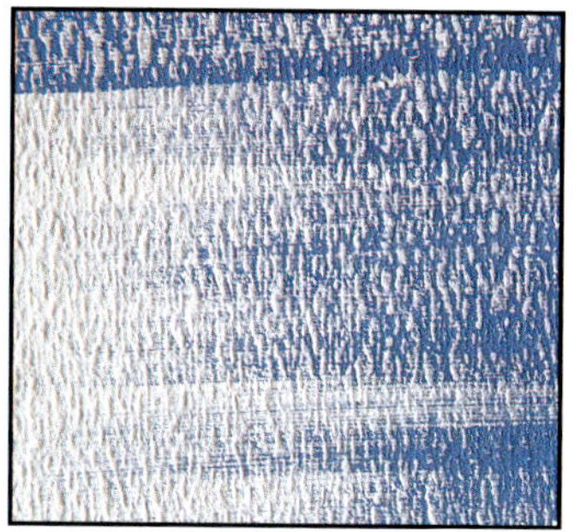

Cold-pressed watercolor paper has less texture than rough and allows for dry-brush techniques.

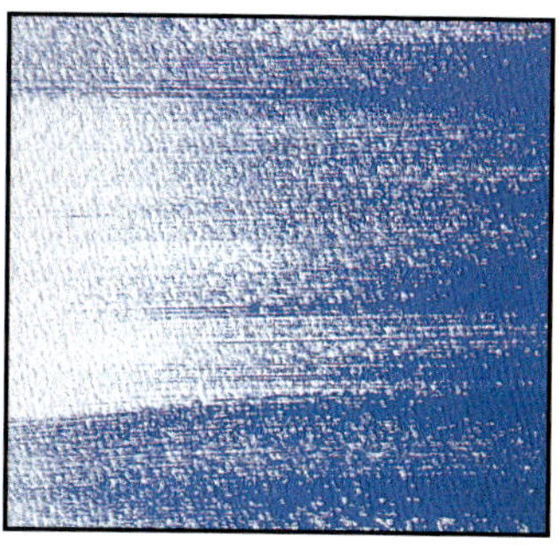

Hot-pressed watercolor paper allows for the greatest detail.

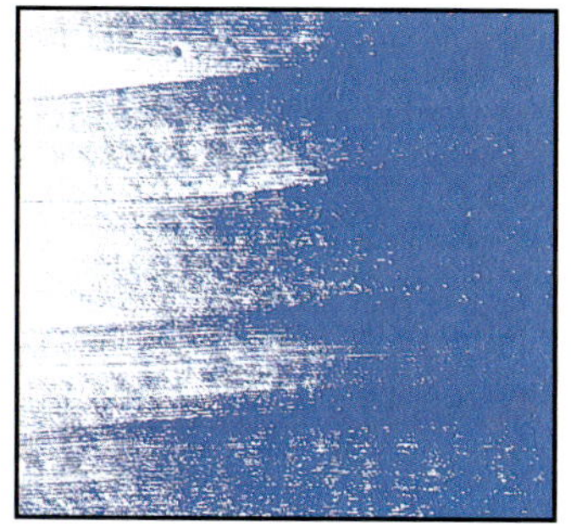

A smooth (hot-pressed) illustration board is the best surface for achieving precise detail. The plate-finish surface feels like an eggshell.

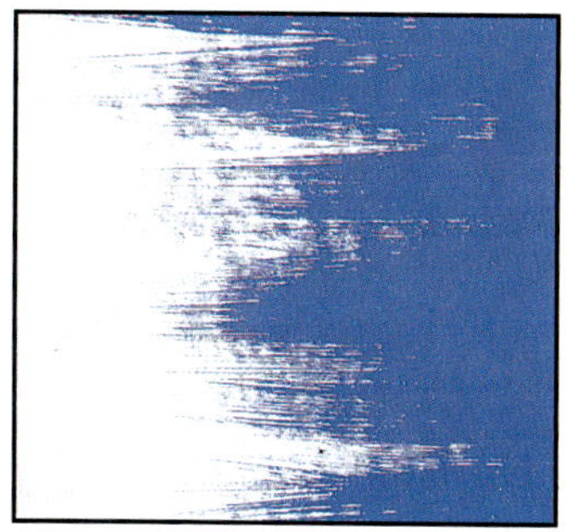

A kid-finish illustration board offers smoothness with a slight tooth. It allows for both dry-brush techniques and excellent detail.

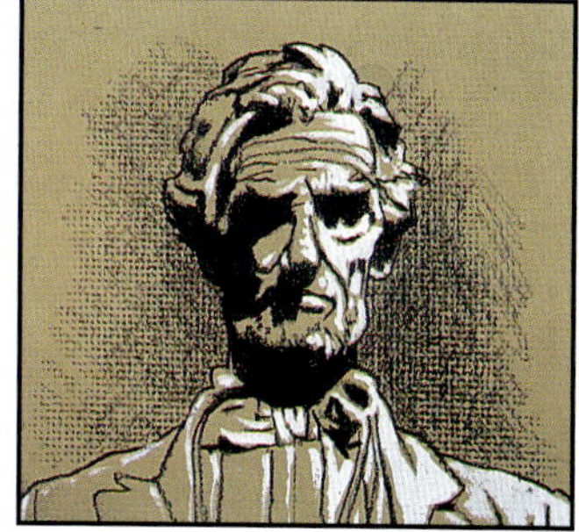

Toned illustration board can be an integral part of the painting. It also works well with charcoal highlighted with white gouache.

Easel or Table?

When painting, you must have a secure platform for the painting surface. Whether to use an easel or table is a personal preference.

Easel

I use a vertical standing easel for several reasons: (1) The easel slants slightly forward at the top, so paint drips onto the floor rather than the painting; (2) it allows me to step away from the painting and view it from a distance; (3) I can view the painting by looking in a large mirror behind my chair, which gives me information I could not see otherwise; (4) it helps to prevent drawing distortion due to foreshortening that you get on a table; and (5) beverages cannot spill on an easel—there's no place to set them.

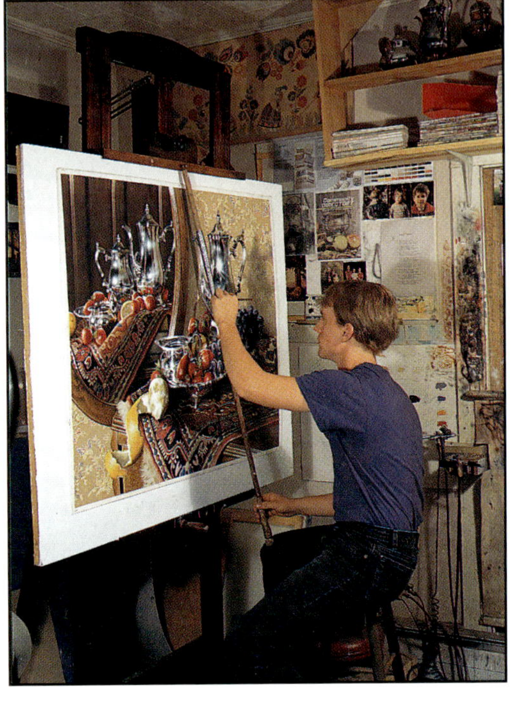

Table

A table is easier on your arms because it allows you to rest them on the painting. You can, however, drag your arm through wet paint or get oil from your hands on the painting. It is best to keep a sheet of tracing paper under your painting arm if you use a table.

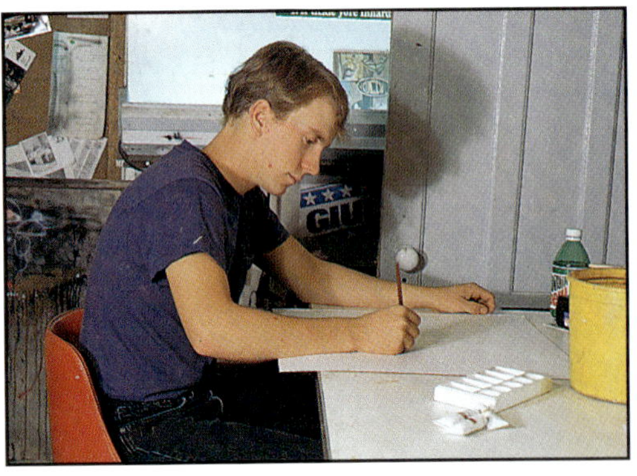

Maulstick

A maulstick is a long, lightweight wood or aluminum dowel used by painters as a rest for the hand while working. The maulstick steadies the painting hand and keeps it away from the painting surface. It also can be used as a guide for painting straight lines. My maulstick is attached to a nail (a screw eye is on the end) at the top of the easel so I can swing it to any position. You can wrap the tip in a soft cloth so it can be placed on the painting surface.

Lighting

The best light is that which simulates daylight. There are many color-balanced lights that will do this. Because I am left handed, I have a row of three bulbs and a row of fluorescent tubes placed behind my right shoulder so my hand doesn't create a shadow when I paint. The bulbs are attached to a white reflector board to create soft indirect lighting.

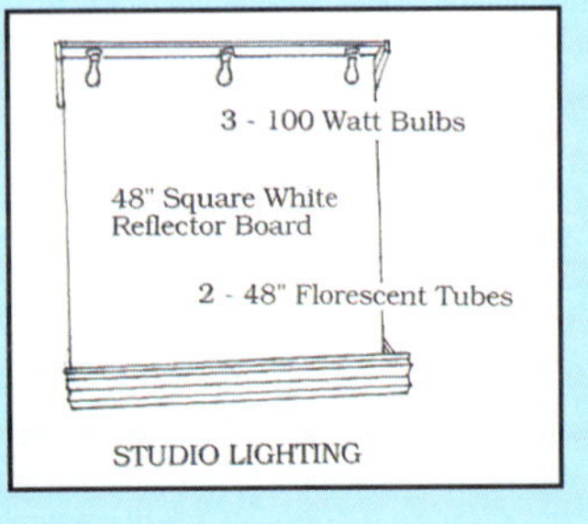

The Drawing

Painting is much easier when you have done the proper groundwork. This involves a complete drawing from which to proceed.

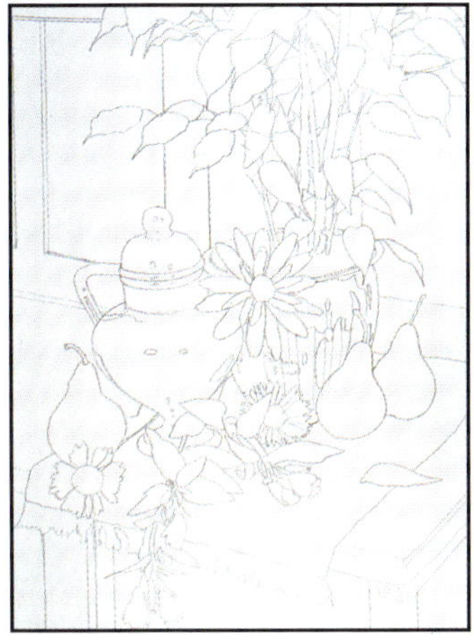

I never begin a piece until I am absolutely sure of what I intend to do with each square inch of the painting surface. It is recommended that you work out the drawing on drawing paper first because erasures can damage the painting surface. Try to get as much information in the pencil drawing as possible. When you are completely satisfied, you can transfer the drawing to the painting surface (see page 10). Important: Be sure to keep your final drawing until the painting is complete.

The Grid System

Artists throughout history have used the grid system to accurately duplicate an image on a painting surface. This system can also be used to enlarge or reduce the image. For example, if you have a photograph that you would like to duplicate, but want to paint it twice as large, you can use the the grid system to draw the subject at 200%.

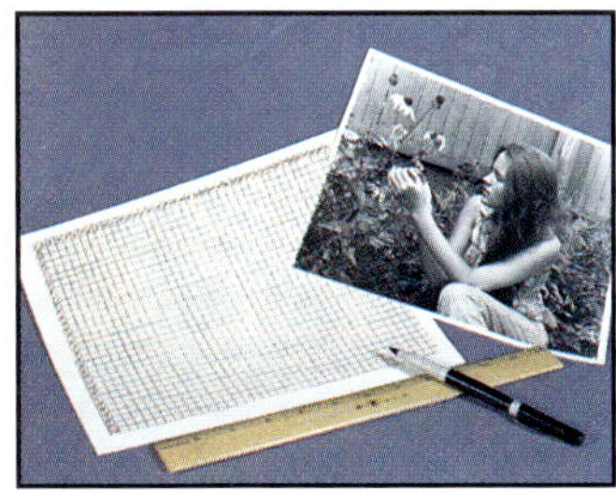

Step 1: Place a piece of acetate over the photograph (or a photocopy), and then use a ruler and fine-tipped marker to draw a 1/2" grid over the photograph.

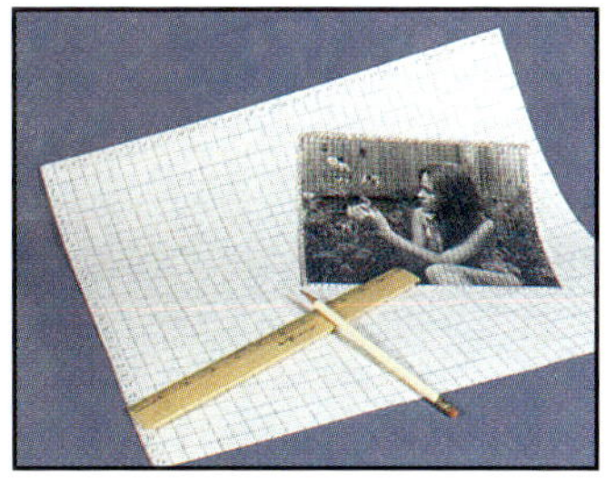

Step 2: Use an HB pencil to lightly draw a 1" grid on the drawing paper. It should have the same number of squares as the grid on the original. The squares can be the same size or reduced or enlarged to the desired size.

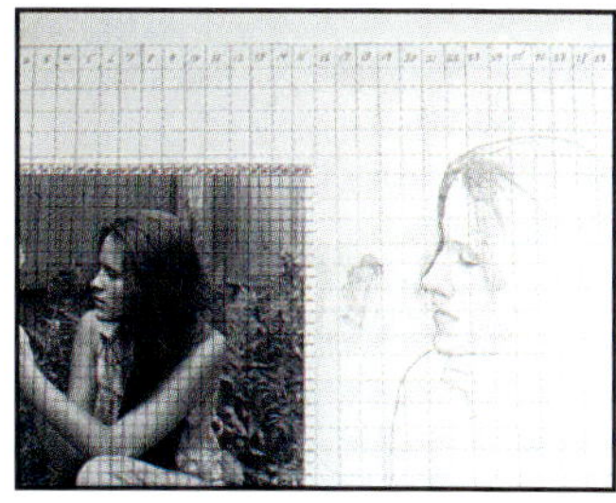

Step 3: Lightly draw the image from each square of the original in the squares on the paper. If desired, number the columns and rows of both grids. The numbers make it easier to draw in the corresponding squares.

Transferring the Drawing

After the drawing is completed on drawing paper, it has to be transferred to the painting support. An easy way to do this is with tracing paper.

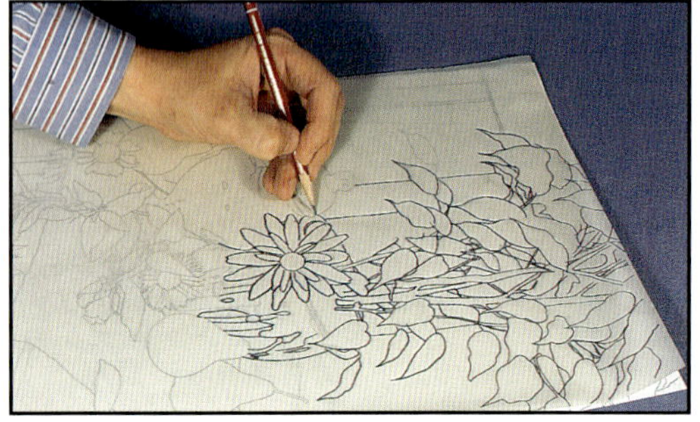

Step 1: Place the tracing paper over the drawing. Either hold the paper in place, or tape it to the drawing board. Carefully trace the entire drawing with an HB pencil.

Note: The lead of an HB pencil is soft, so it is important to keep your hand from smudging the drawing.

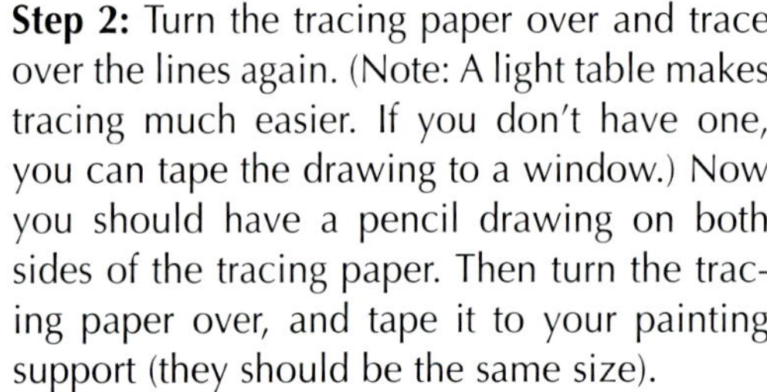

Step 2: Turn the tracing paper over and trace over the lines again. (Note: A light table makes tracing much easier. If you don't have one, you can tape the drawing to a window.) Now you should have a pencil drawing on both sides of the tracing paper. Then turn the tracing paper over, and tape it to your painting support (they should be the same size).

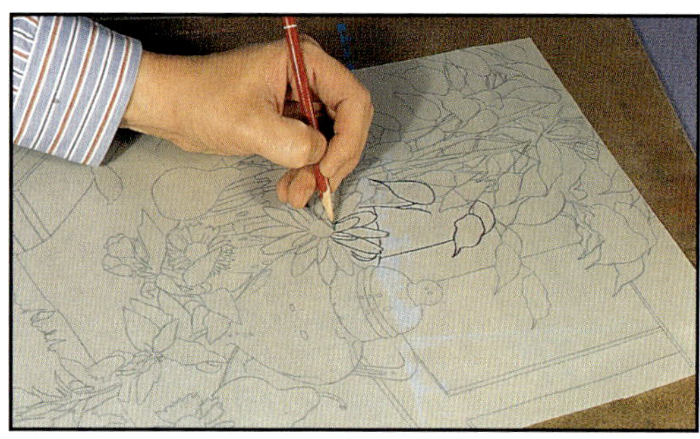

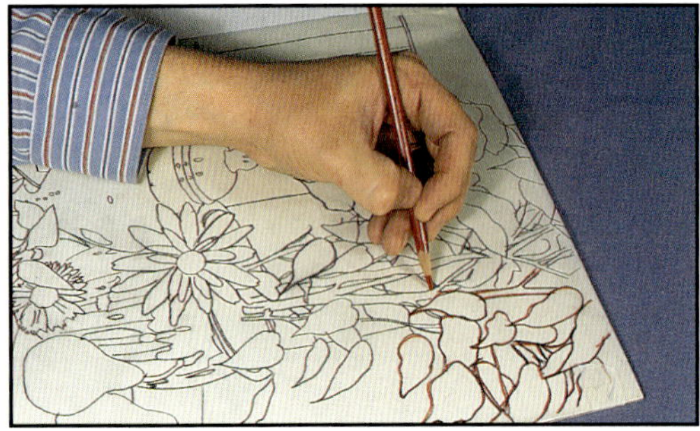

Step 3: Retrace the entire drawing with a colored pencil to transfer the graphite on the back of the paper to the painting surface. The colored pencil enables you to see which lines you have already traced over. Thus, if interrupted, you'll be able to see where you stopped.

Projection

Another way to transfer an image is to project it onto the painting surface and then lightly trace over it with an HB pencil. There are three different devices that can be used for projection: (1) the opaque projector, which can project an opaque image, such as a photograph or drawing; (2) the overhead transparency projector, which works well with black, white, or inked drawings transferred to acetate on a copy machine; and (3) the slide projector.

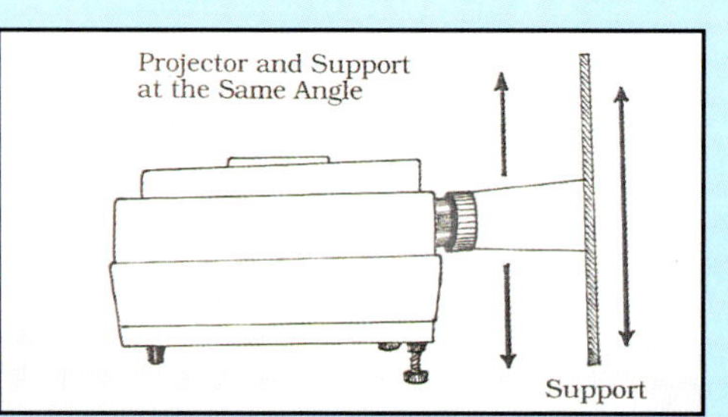

Ensure that the angle of the projector is parallel with the angle of the support or the image will appear distorted. The edges of the projected image should be parallel with the edges of the support.

Drawing Dark over Light/Light over Dark

One of the advantages of gouache is its unique covering power—but the paint needs to be controlled carefully so that you don't lose your drawing beneath it. There are a number of effective ways do this.

Drawing Dark over Light

One way to keep a drawing from being lost when painted over with gouache is to first paint the background and then use the tracing paper method (see page 10) to transfer the drawing onto the completed background.

For example, if you are painting a farm scene, you could paint the sky, and then redraw the buildings over the sky you've painted. You could also paint around the buildings. (To paint around a tree, however, is impractical.) Another approach is to ink over the drawing and paint over it with light washes. This way, you can still see the drawing through the paint. Thinned acrylics can also be used to define the drawing. Generally, I paint around things, but if I cover the drawing, I redefine it by using the tracing paper method.

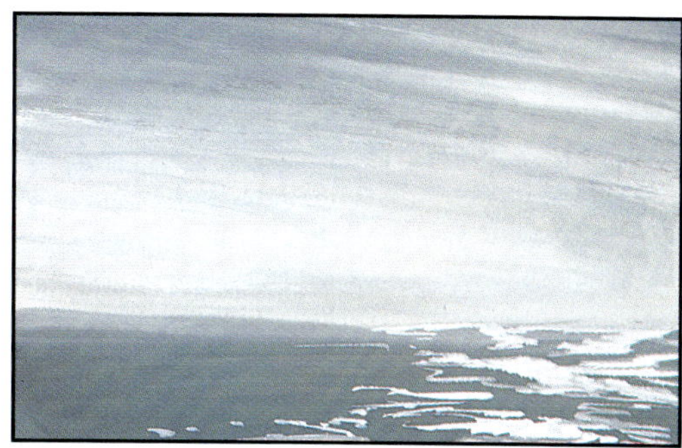

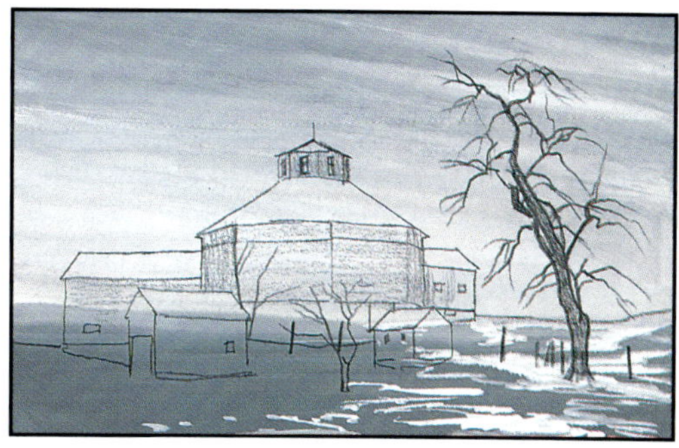

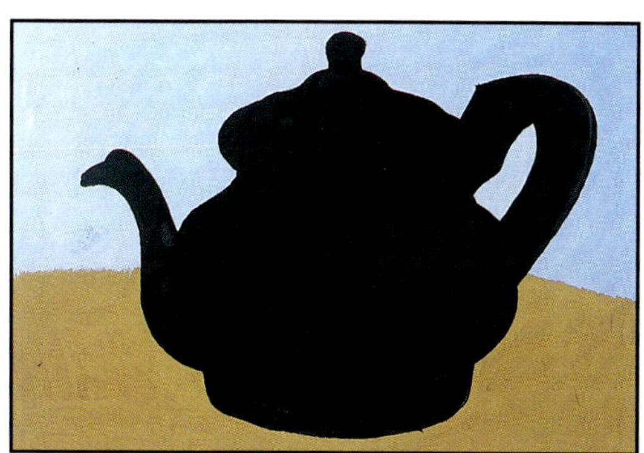

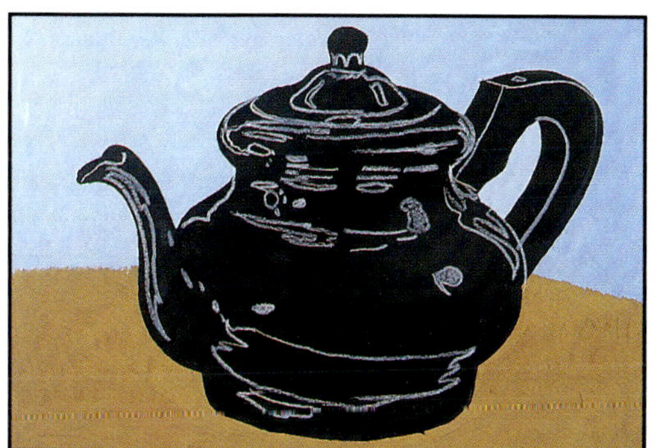

Drawing Light over Dark

Gouache is great for working from dark to light colors. For example, when painting silver objects, I paint them pure back, then dark gray, light gray, lightest gray, and, finally, pure white. To those who have never used gouache, it may seem strange to paint in this order, but this is the easiest and most effective way to use gouache.

When painting an object completely black, you'll lose the drawing underneath, but this is not a problem. You can use the tracing paper method to retrace the drawing; however, you will coat the back of the drawing with light-colored chalk or pastel or white charcoal. The lighter color will transfer onto the dark gouache underpainting, restoring the original drawing in full detail. (Note the importance of keeping the final drawing until the painting is finished.)

Gouache

Gouache, a French term meaning "opaque," is simply opaque watercolor paint. Its brightness comes from the color itself—unlike transparent watercolor, which gets its brilliance from the reflective qualities of the paper. Gouache can be used thinly, like transparent watercolors, but it is generally used as a matte, opaque paint. Gouache provides an actual paint layer, while transparent watercolor is a stain. Often referred to as "body color," the film of gouache appears thicker than it really is.

What It Is

Gouache is made from pigment, binder (usually gum arabic), wetting agents, other minor additives, and a preservative. More pigment is used in making gouache than transparent watercolors, which makes them opaque. An opaque extender (aluminum hydrate, blanc fixe, or precipitated chalk) is also added to the transparent pigments to make them even more opaque and improve the handling qualities. Precipitated chalk is added to some of the duller pigments to brighten them. It is best to use professional-grade paints; cheaper gouache paints are made from inferior ingredients, tend to crack, and are not as permanent as high-grade paints.

To ensure that the painting will last a long while—even longer than an oil painting—use quality gouache on an acid-free paper and display it unvarnished behind glass. There is nothing in gouache that will yellow. Of all the mediums available, there is nothing that compares with the opacity, quick drying time, and ability to achieve minute detail as gouache.

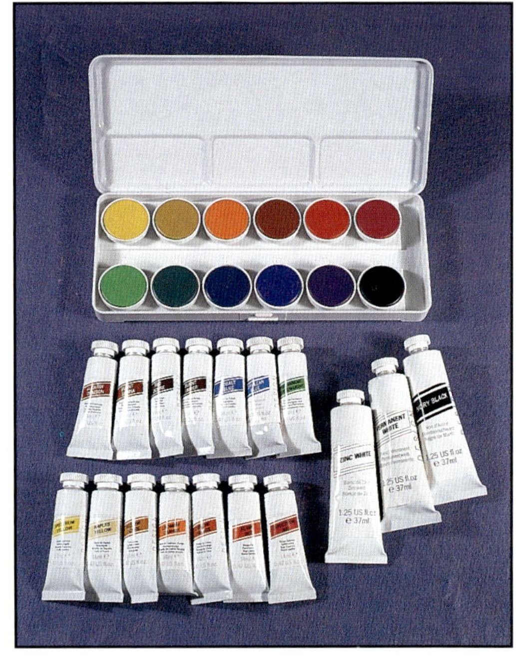

Gouache is available in tubes and cakes, but cakes are neither as bright nor as practical as the tube colors.

A Brief History

The history of gouache is hazy at best. Ancient Egyptians, Greeks, and Romans painted with the precursor of modern gouache. During the Middle Ages it was used to illuminate (illustrate) manuscripts. The masters often used white gouache to highlight their drawings, which were done on toned supports. Between the 16th and 18th centuries, gouache was popular for miniature painting. During the 18th century, it was used by watercolorists in Italy, France, and Switzerland. In the 19th century, gouache was used in conjunction with traditional watercolors for special effects. Great artists who have used gouache include Dürer, Van Gogh, Poussin, Toulouse-Lautrec, Picasso, Miró, Rouault, and Shahn.

How to Use Gouache

Remember this phrase: "Dark colors dry lighter, light colors dry darker." Gouache changes as it dries, so take into account the slight color shift. Also, it is good practice to always mix extra paint; this way, it will be ready when you need it. (Gouache can be stored for several weeks. Baby food jars make perfect containers.)

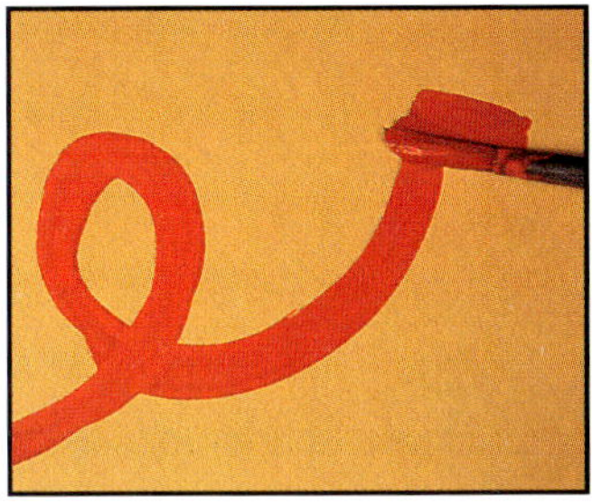

The proper consistency for gouache is similar to heavy cream; it should brush out easily. With practice, you will be able to mix the proper consistency every time.

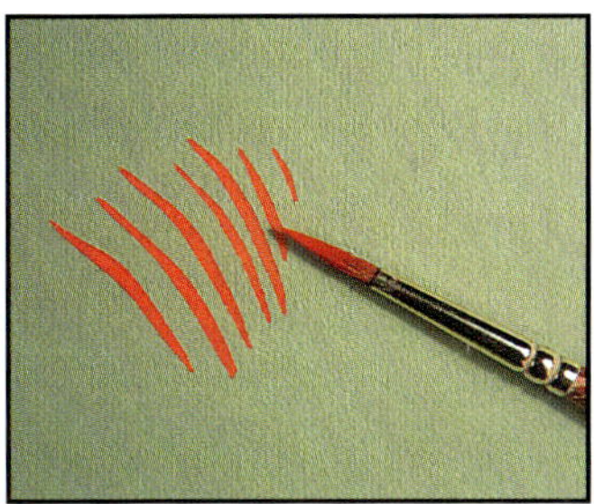

Load the tip of the brush—rather than the entire head—with paint. This helps to create fine lines and have greater control. Wipe off excess paint with a paper towel.

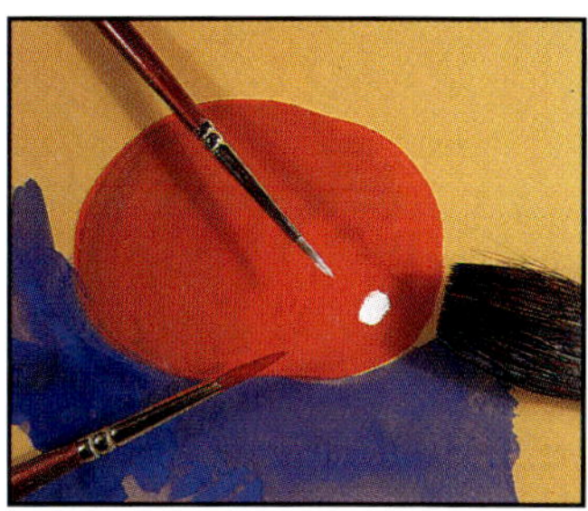

Use the proper brush for the proper job—large brushes for large areas, medium brushes for medium areas, and small brushes for small areas.

Things to Avoid

Overdiluted gouache—Generally, gouache is meant to be used opaquely.

Flimsy surfaces—A painting surface that buckles, bends, or is too thin can cause the paint to chip and crack.

Dirty rinse water for brushes—Keeping the water clean will maximize the brilliance of your paints.

Designer colors—Pigments with fancy names, such as "peacock blue" or "bengal rose," were used originally for design work. They were not meant to be permanent. Stick to traditional colors and don't use fugitive colors (those that fade in light).

Cheap brands of paint—Poor-quality gouache will shift dramatically from the wet to the dry state. Artist-grade paints will last longer.

Worn brushes—For quality brush strokes and clean lines, use brushes that are in good condition.

Cheap brushes—They are bad from the start and will cause much frustration. Always buy the best brushes that you can afford.

Overexposure—Avoid displaying your paintings in direct sunlight or under fluorescent lighting. Ultra-violet (UV) light will cause some colors to fade.

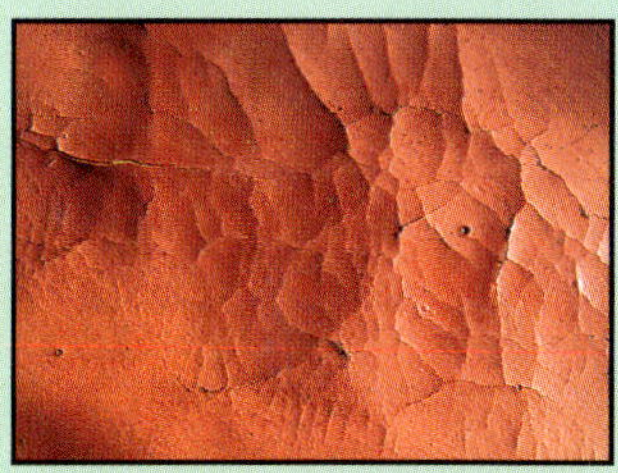

Gouache applied too thickly may crack. Use it in a creamy fashion—not in thick, heavy layers.

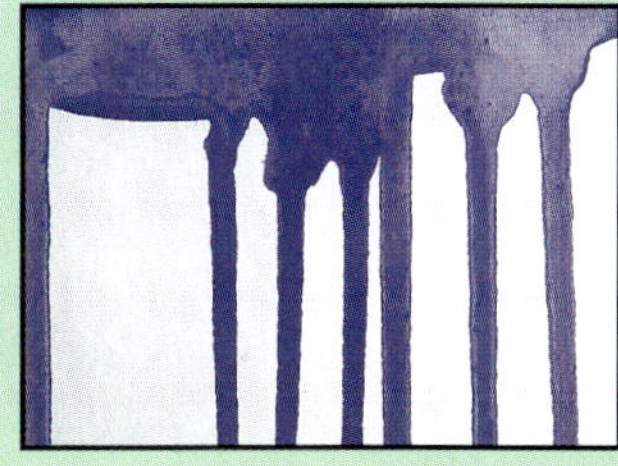

Applied too thinly, gouache will run, creating drips and other unwanted effects.

Gouache Painting Techniques

Gouache can be used in many different ways and manipulated to produce various effects.

Applied evenly with a large brush, gouache is perfect for creating straight, flat areas of color. Adding ox gall to the diluent water will help to achieve a perfect surface.

Gouache can be applied with a large flat watercolor brush to create subtle, beautiful gradations of color. This yellow-red combination was done with a large, soft-hair brush.

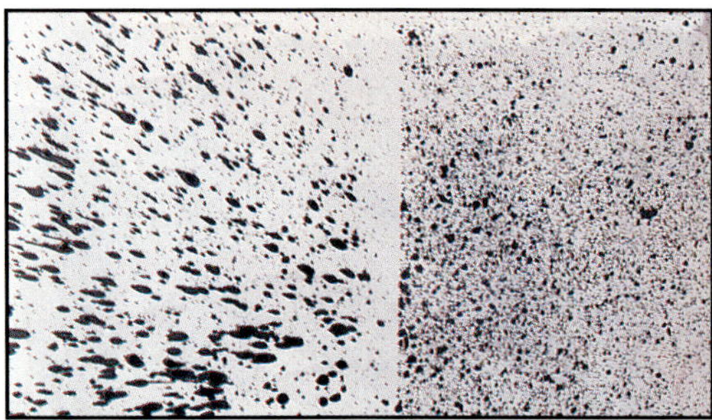

Spattering can be done with a bristle brush (left) or a toothbrush (right). Load the brush with gouache, shake it to get rid of excess paint, and then pull back the bristles with your fingers. Spattering creates texture on surfaces such as rock, wood, or ceramic.

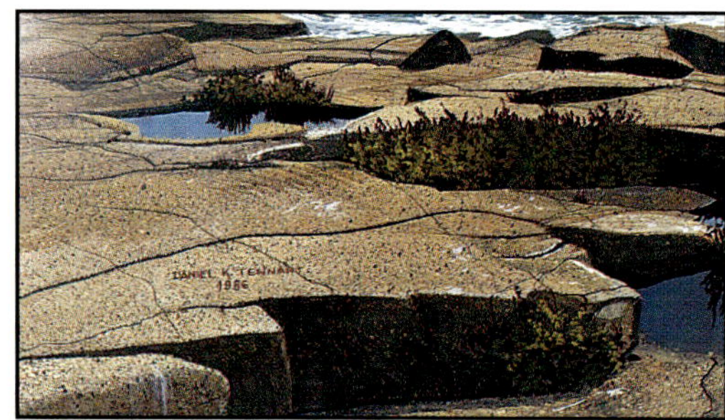

In this portion of the painting, spattering was used in a highly realistic manner. The foreground rocks were speckled with different colors. The spattering technique made them very persuasive. As with any painting technique, don't overdo it or it will look gimmicky.

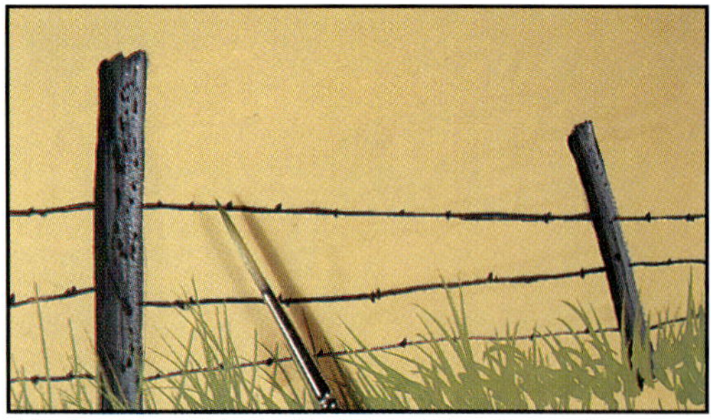

With a fully loaded rigger brush on hot-pressed illustration board, the brush glides along, making thin, opaque stroke lines. The rigger works well for painting wood grains, grasses, telephone wire, barbed wire fencing, or any thing that requires a long, fine line.

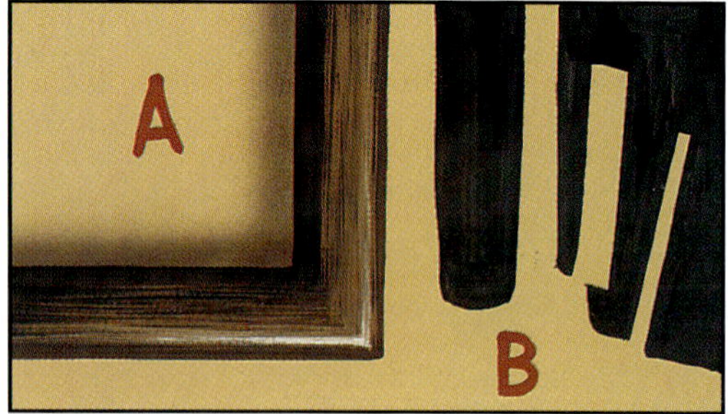

Masking an area with drafting tape is an excellent technique for creating straight lines. Side A shows a picture frame painted using tape along the edges. Side B shows the negative spaces created by placing tape, painting the background, and then removing the tape.

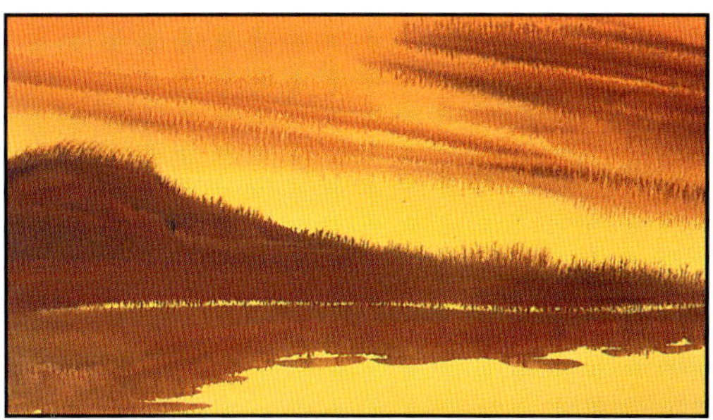

Although gouache was not made to be used in thin washes, it can be an effective technique. When thinned, some of the more transparent pigments will rival transparent watercolors.

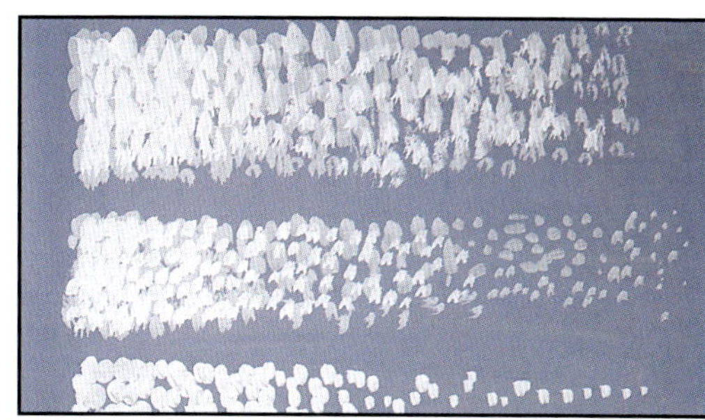

Stippling means to apply the paint with dots or light touches of the brush. This adds texture and interest while still allowing the underpainting to show through.

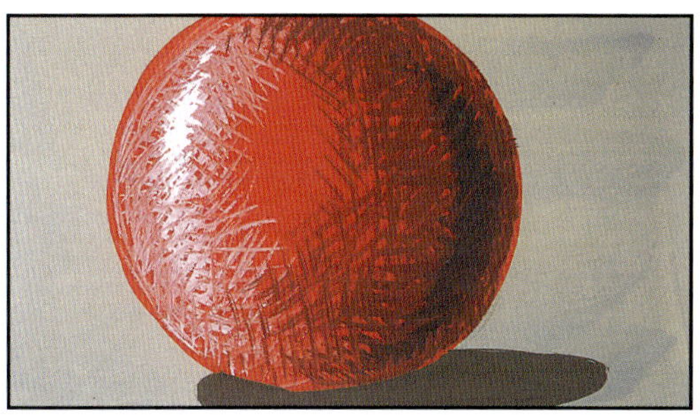

Crosshatching is a good way to blend gouache because it dries quickly. Load the very tip of the brush with paint, wipe off the excess, and then apply in light strokes, weaving (warp and woof) with vertical, horizontal, and diagonal strokes.

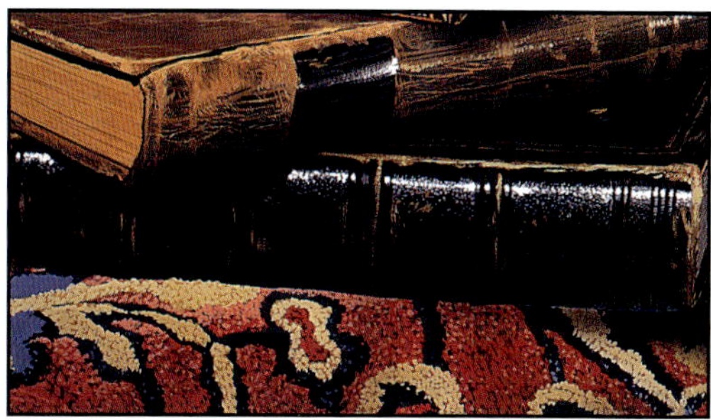

This is an example of stippling to create the illusion of carpet and textured book binding. The black book was painted black, and then dark gray was stippled over the black. Light gray was stippled over the dark gray, and then final highlights of white were stippled.

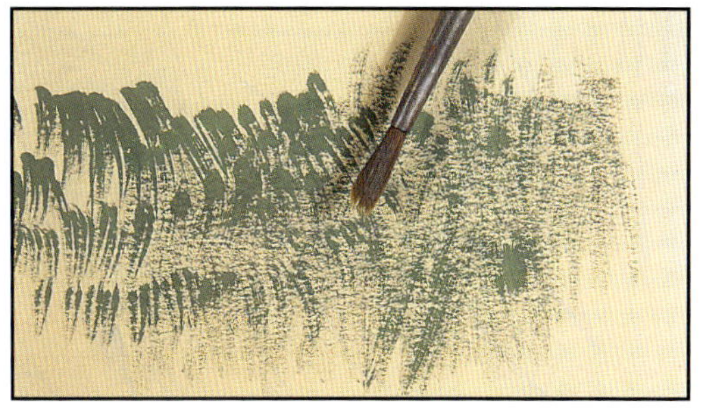

The drybrush technique is somewhat self-explanatory. Load a red sable brush with paint, and then squeeze it until it is almost dry. Spread the hairs of the brush as you squeeze it. This creates the same effect as using a very small brush to make parallel lines.

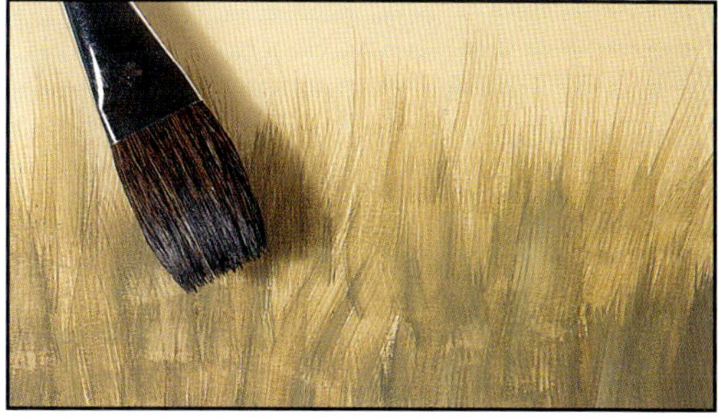

Drybrushing with a larger brush gives the same effect as the red sable but on a larger scale. This technique is helpful in painting foregrounds that have weeds and grasses in them. It also works well with dried weeds in winter scenes and texture on wood and cloth.

The Airbrush

The airbrush is a small pen-sized tool that uses compressed air to spray paint. It was invented in 1893 by Charles Burdick, whose original intention was to use it for watercolor painting. It became popular, however, for photo retouching, and, for many years, it continued to be used mainly in the graphic arts field. It has only been in the past 30 years that the airbrush has entered into a new major role—as a tool for the fine artist. The airbrush is an excellent tool for artists who want to expand their working capabilities. It extends the possibilities and effects of any medium that can be sprayed through it. There are some effects—such as fog, controlled spattering, delicate blendings, glazes with watercolor—that would be impossible to achieve without the airbrush.

Single Action vs. Double Action

Single action and double action describe the trigger controls of the airbrush. An airbrush is either one or the other (except for the oscillating type, which is in a category by itself). With a single-action model, both air and paint come out when you press down on the trigger. The paint spray is changed by adjusting the screw on the back of the handle (on some models). You have to stop painting to adjust the amount of spray. With a double-action model, when you push down on the trigger you get air, and by pushing down and pulling back, you get air and paint. The farther back you pull, the more paint you get. The double-action airbrush is preferred because it provides more control.

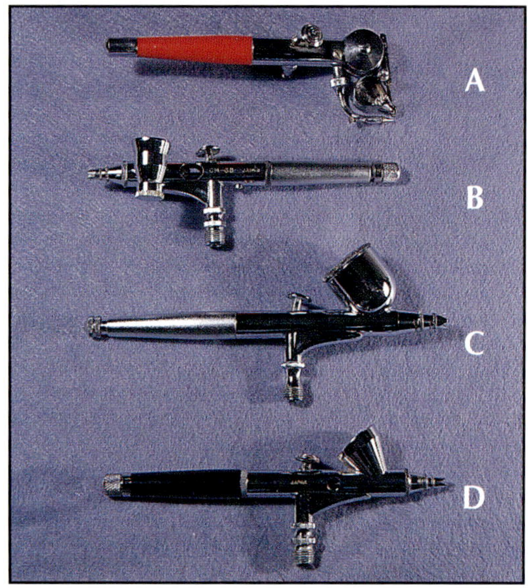

(A) *oscillating model*—provides the finest spray; (B) *side cup, double-action model*—allows for quick color changes; (C) *large, gravity-fed cup model*—holds a lot of paint; (D) *gravity-fed model*—has a very fine spray.

External Mix vs. Internal Mix

With an external-mix airbrush, air and paint are mixed (atomization) outside the body of the airbrush. With an internal-mix model, they are mixed inside the body. The internal mix is recommended because it creates a much finer spray and does not create large dots of paint. The external-mix models have a grittier spray. In general, less-expensive hobby airbrushes are external mix. All professional, double-action airbrushes are internal mix.

How to Start Airbrushing

The airbrush should be advanced enough that you can grow into it. Again, a double-action, internal-mix model is recommended. The air hose is necessary to give pressure to the airbrush. Purchase whatever type is recommended for your airbrush and compressor. The compressor is the most important consideration. You will airbrush at 30–40 pounds per square inch (PSI). PSI is the pressure at which air flows through the airbrush. If the pressure is too high, the paint will be hard to control; if too weak, the paint will hardly come out. A good compressor will have a pressure regulator that automatically keeps the air pressure constant. For paint, you will use thinned gouache. It should be the consistency of milk—or slightly heavier. If it is too thick, it will come out in spatters; if too thin, it will run.

Elements of Airbrushing

There are four essential elements for airbrushing—an airbrush, air hose, compressor, and paint. Your budget will dictate your selections. Keep in mind that, when properly cared for, good-quality supplies will last a lifetime.

Respirators

You must protect your lungs while airbrushing. Paint can ricochet off the support and become airborne. You can see it and, on occasion, even taste it. Hence, the necessity of a respirator. A respirator fits over your mouth and nose and filters out minute particles of paint. There are different kinds of filters available. The more expensive types have charcoal filters and filtering pads so they are especially safe. Make sure you buy the proper respirator for watercolor and gouache.

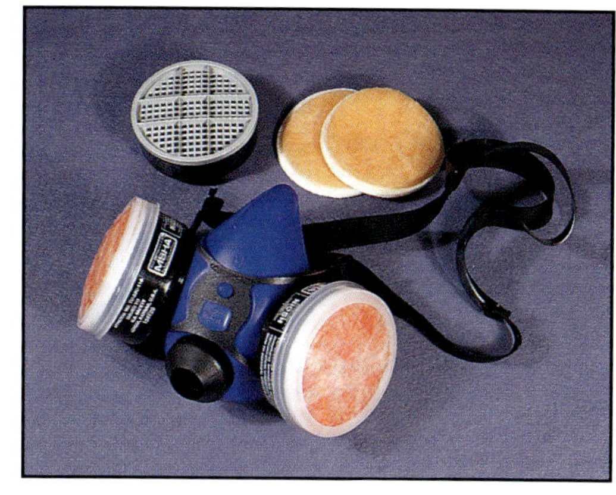

Compressors and Air Sources

Compressors are the most popular sources of air power. Run by small motors that range from 1/16- to 1/2-horse power, they run either "silently" or continuously. A silent compressor has a storage tank, and, when it reaches the proper PSI, it shuts off. You can spray in silence until the pressure drops and the motor has to maintain the pressure. The smaller, continuous-running compressors are noisy and not as powerful. The silent compressor is the most expensive model but highly recommended for a lifetime of use. Some of the larger compressors are oil free, which are maintenance free, and also highly recommended.

Another type of air source is the CO_2 tank. These are large tanks of compressed carbon dioxide. They last for quite a while but eventually have to be refilled. They can be refilled at scuba or party supply shops. Many art studios prefer CO_2 tanks because they are so quiet.

The third option—but not a practical one—is the "canned air" sold at art stores. Canned air is quite expensive for what you get. The pressure in one can of air will probably not last long enough for one major project.

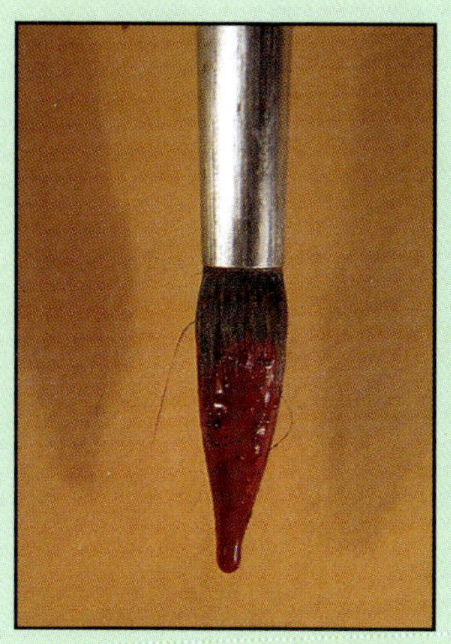

Preparing the Paint

Gouache should have the consistency of milk to flow smoothly through the airbrush. To test for the proper thickness, use the "drip technique." Load a brush full of paint, and watch how the paint drips off the brush. It should drip at a steady rate—not a rapid, "drip-drip-drip," like water, nor a slow drip, like pudding. After a few tries, you will be able to tell if the paint is too thin or thick simply by the sound of the dripping.

If gouache dries in the airbrush, simply fill the color holder with warm water, let it sit for 5 minutes, and then blow the water out. If bits of gouache do not dissolve readily, use a toothpick to ream them out. Don't use anything metallic because it can scratch the airbrush.

Airbrushing Exercises

Using the airbrush is not difficult, but it requires practice to master. Each of these exercises is designed for a specific skill. Practice each exercise daily and you will become proficient.

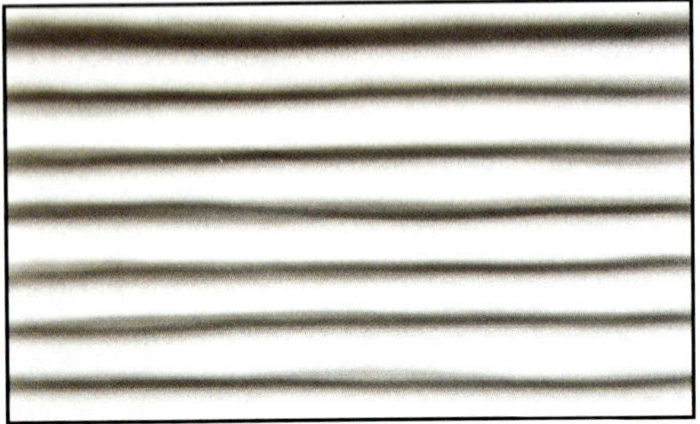

Practicing parallel lines freehand is important for line control. Practice the motion of keeping the lines from touching each other and making them consistent in thickness.

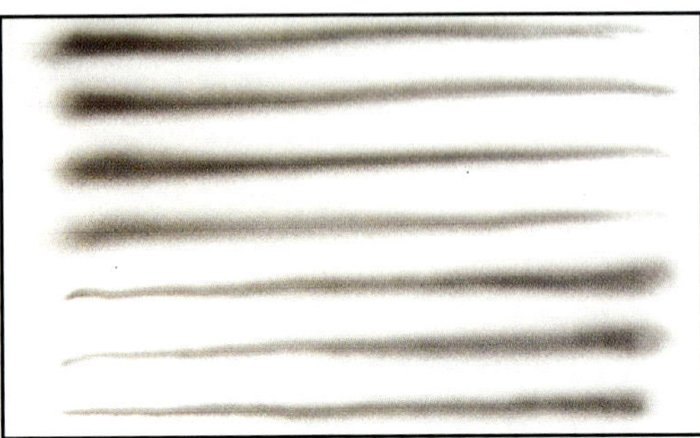

In this exercise, begin spraying the line while holding the tool close to the paper. As you continue, gradually pull the airbrush farther away, creating a thicker, softer line.

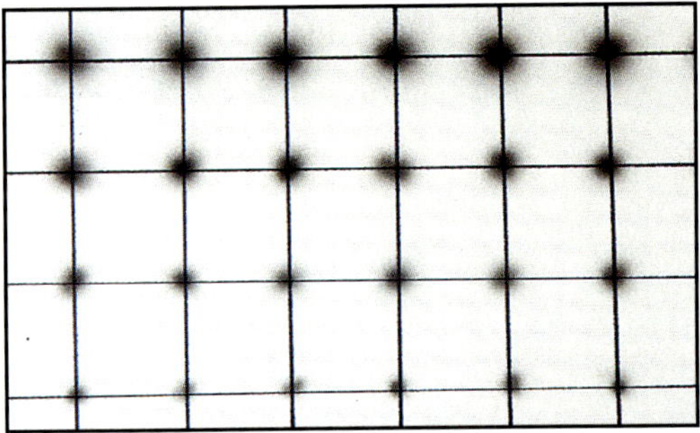

The farther away the airbrush is from the paper, the larger the spray. Make large dots at the top, medium dots in the middle, and small dots at the bottom.

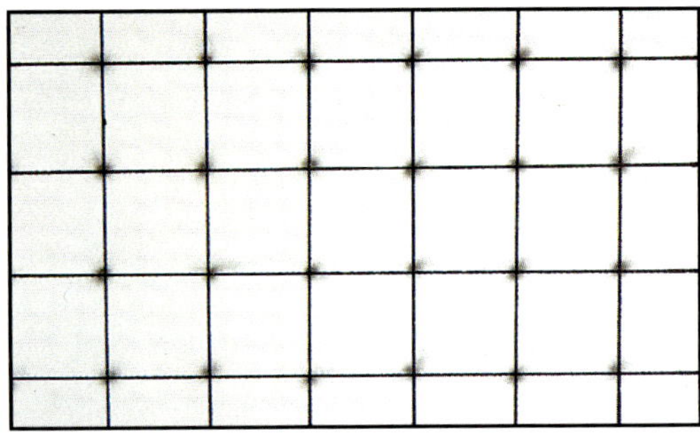

Try making dots of the same size at each intersection of the grid. When you can make the same-sized dots, you will know that you have good control of the airbrush.

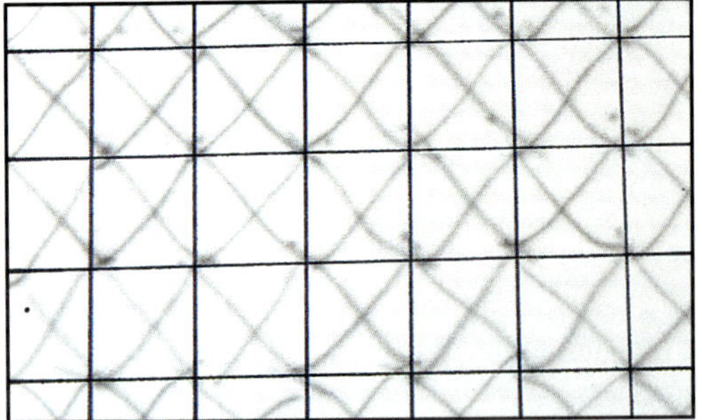

Making Xs across the paper will test your eye–hand coordination and ability to make even stroke lines with a quick stop. Remember, the end result is not as important as testing the capabilities of the airbrush.

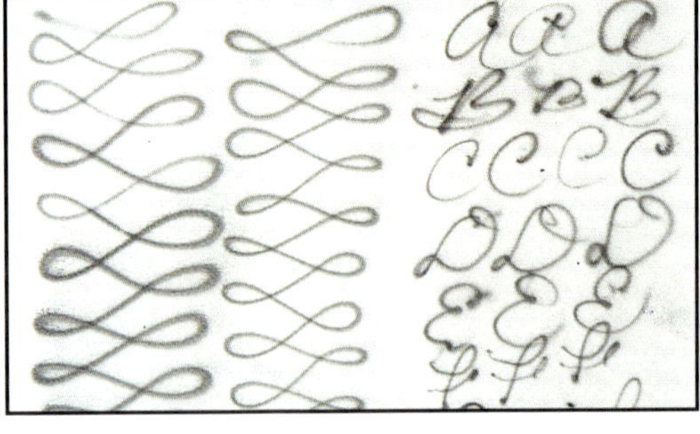

Making curlicues and writing in cursive are good techniques for developing coordination.

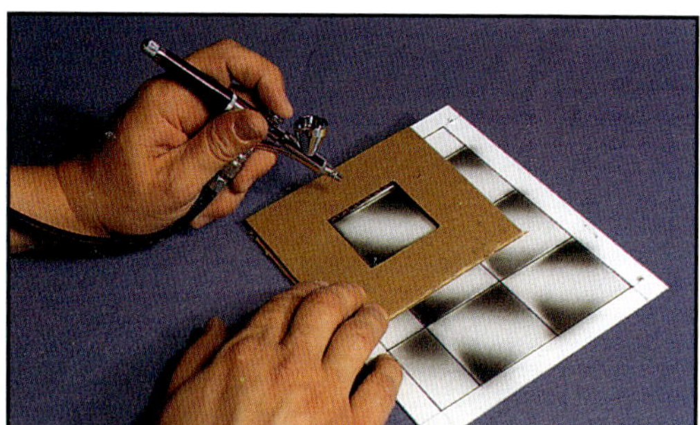

To create a metallic effect, first cut a 2" square stencil out of cardboard. Then place the stencil over the paper and spray black gouache at a diagonal in two opposite corners.

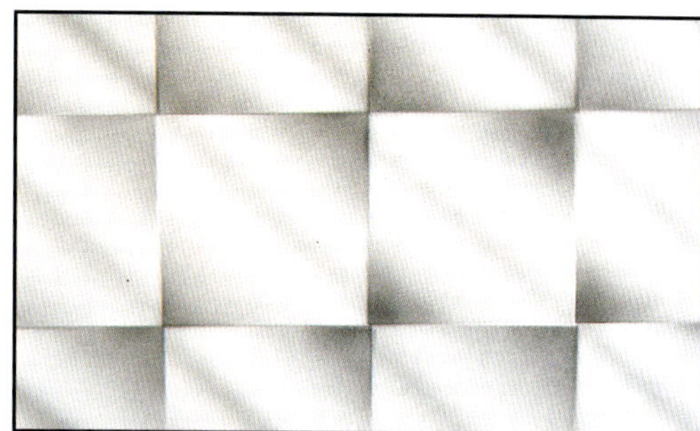

There should be a light strip of plain paper left in the middle of each square. When you are finished with the exercise, the paper should look like a panel of metallic squares.

Spraying a graduated color from top to bottom—or vice versa—is a technique used to create backgrounds, skies, or anything that requires gradual blending.

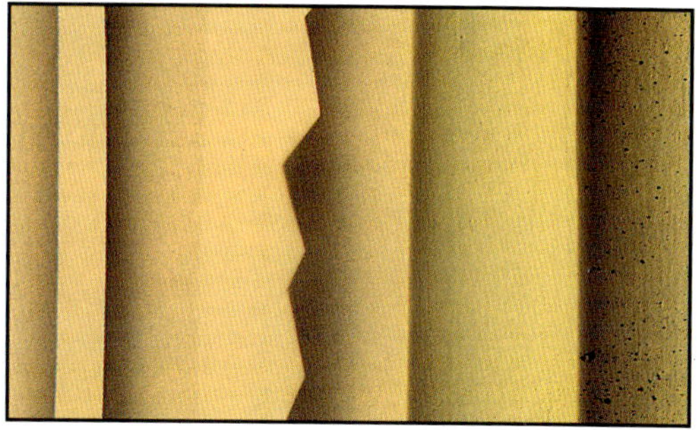

Create hard edges by placing various objects directly on the paper. Here, drafting tape, a piece of paper, a ruler, and a piece of cardboard have been used to create hard edges.

You can achieve soft edges by spraying over items that are elevated off the paper. The overspray softens the edges. Use paper, rulers, cardboard, or cotton to create soft edges.

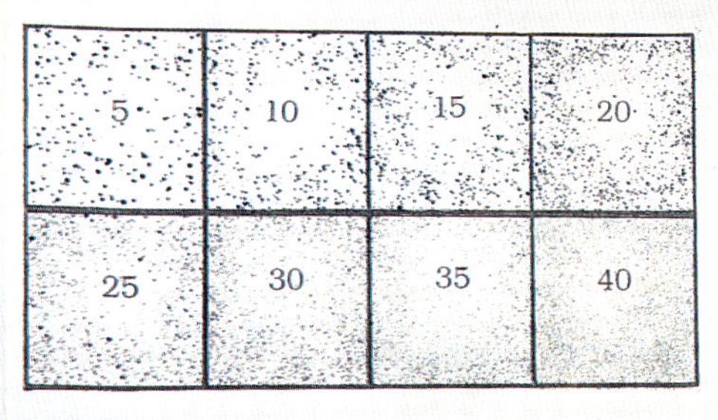

The dot size of the spray depends on the PSI setting. The lower the pressure, the larger the dot pattern. Note: This effect can only be done with airbrushes that have a spatter capability.

Stenciling

There are two ways to paint with an airbrush—freehand or with stencils. Each method provides a different look. Freehand techniques are excellent for producing soft shadows, mellow gradations, and soft, fine lines. Stencils work well for items that have hard edges, straight lines, or areas where precision is required.

Stencils provide complete control of the spray; there is no guesswork with this technique. There are various types of stenciling material and different ways of using them. Here, a piece of frosted stencil film has been laid over a painting in progress, and the stencil is being cut out with a very sharp art knife.

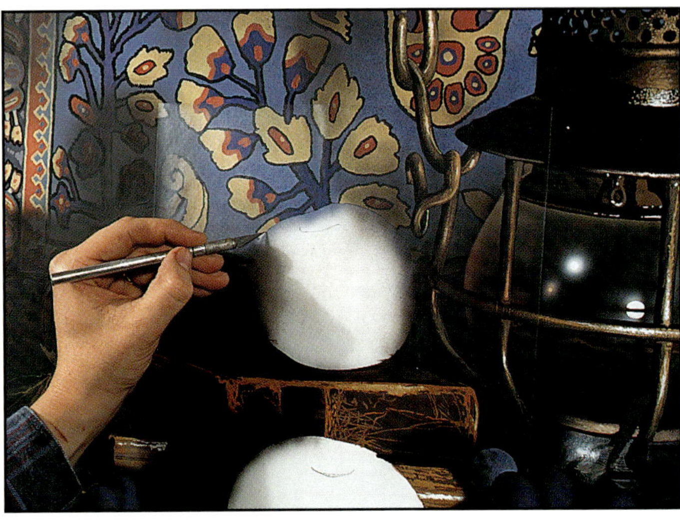

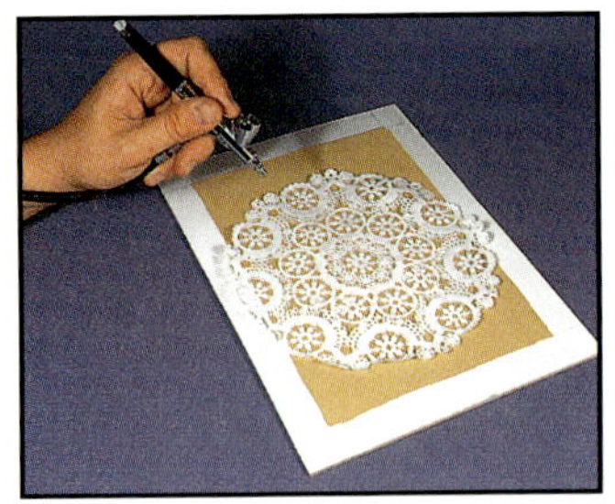

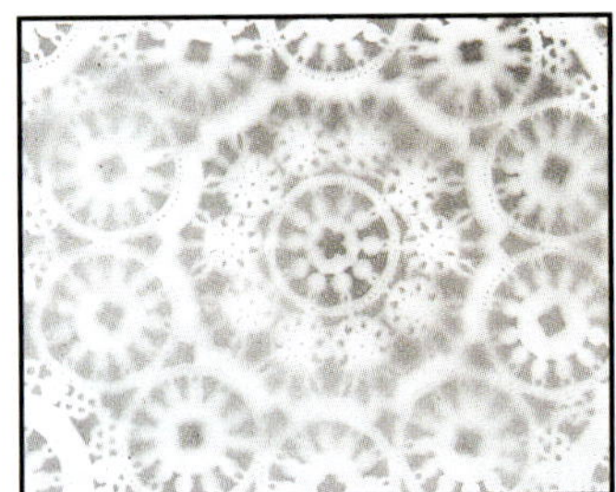

Ordinary objects can also be used as stencils, such as a piece of lace or a cloth doily. First lay the object flat on the support. Spray directly down at the cloth. Wait for the paint to dry, and then lift the object off the support.

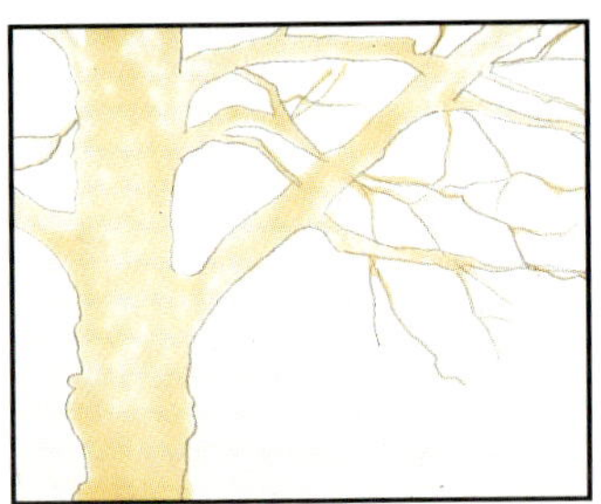

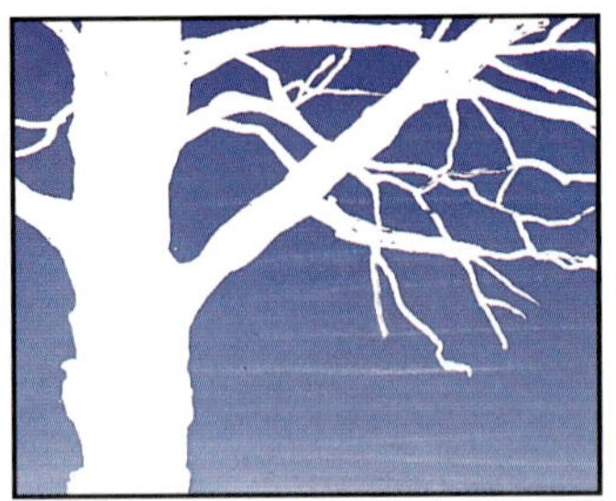

Apply liquid masking fluid with a soaped brush. When the fluid is dry, you can paint over it. When the paint is dry, remove the masking fluid by rubbing it. Wherever the fluid was applied, the paper will be intact and untouched.

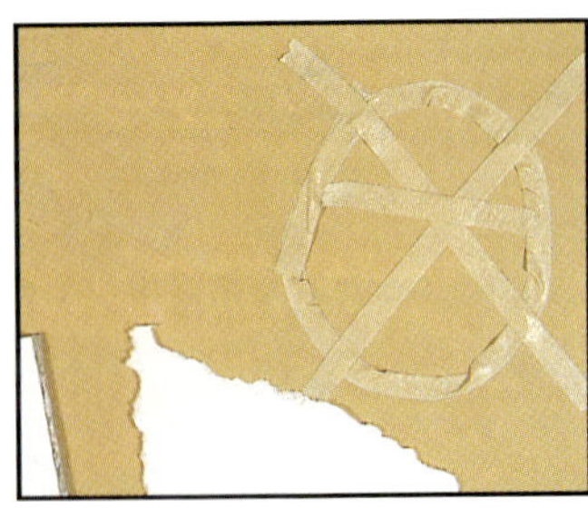

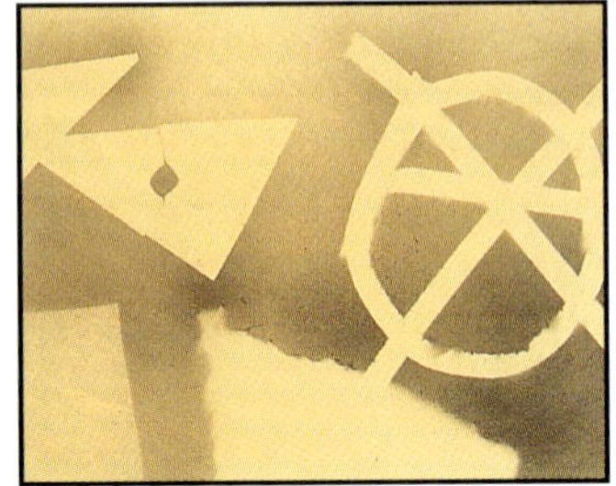

Use torn paper patterns to create unusual images. The farther away the paper is from the painting, the softer the pattern. The closer it is, the crisper the edges. Stencils can be made from tape, paper, cotton, or cardboard.

Airbrushing Basic Forms

The four basic forms—sphere, cylinder, cube, cone—have been recognized as the four elements (singular or combined) that make up almost anything an artist draws or paints.

Sphere

Step 1: Draw the sphere in pencil, overlay it with stenciling film, and then cut with an x-acto knife.

Step 2: Remove the center of the stencil and spray the edges and right side.

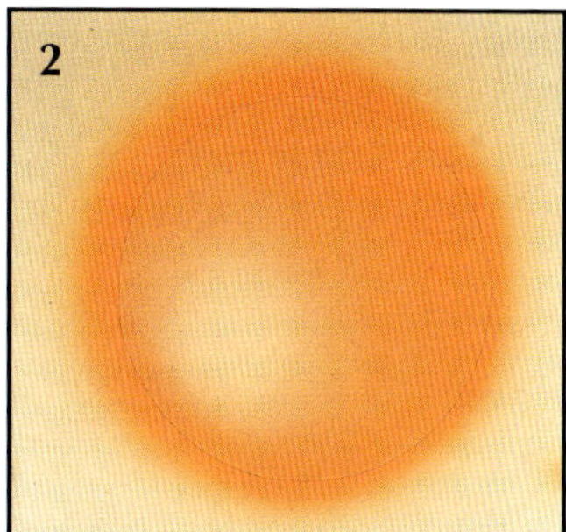

Step 3: Spray the right-hand side of the sphere to create shading with ivory black watercolor.

Step 4: Spray a white highlight in the proper spot to add interest and shape. Then remove the stencil.

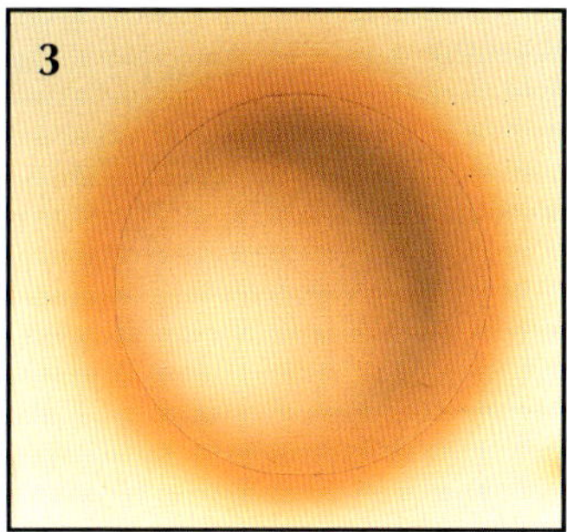

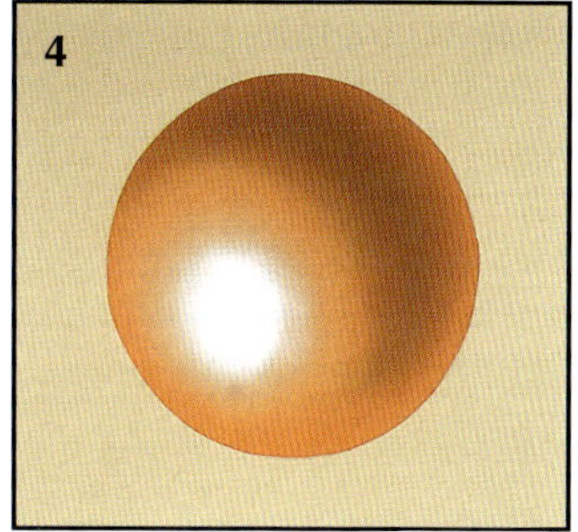

Cube

Step 1: Draw the cube and overlay it with stenciling film. Then make cutouts and number them in the order they will be sprayed.

Step 2: Remove the first cutout, and then airbrush that side of the cube.

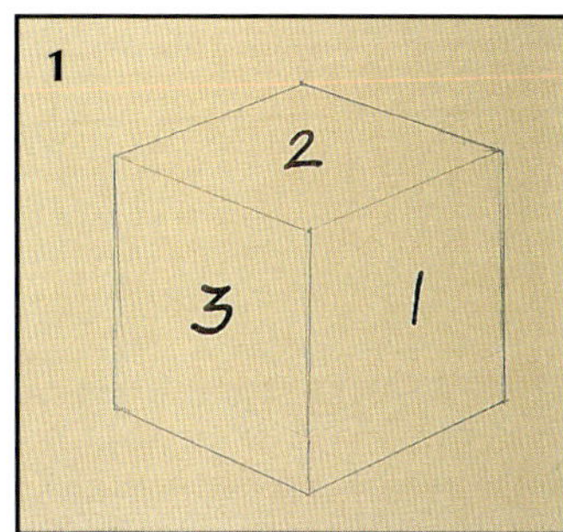

Step 3: Remove the second cutout; then spray the first and second cutouts, creating two degrees of darkness.

Step 4: Spray the third cutout lightly, creating a cube that appears to be three-dimensional. Remove the stencil.

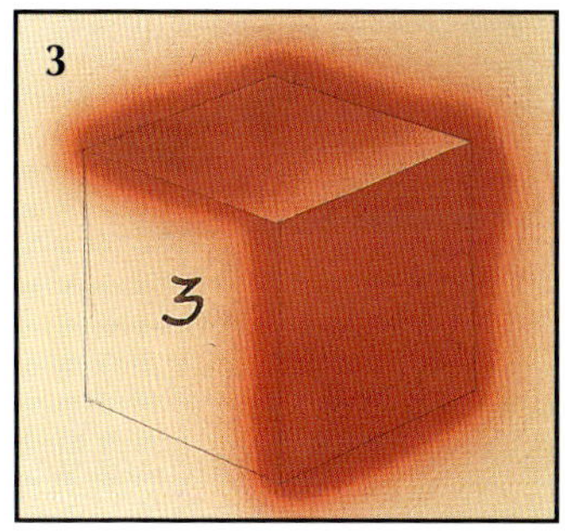

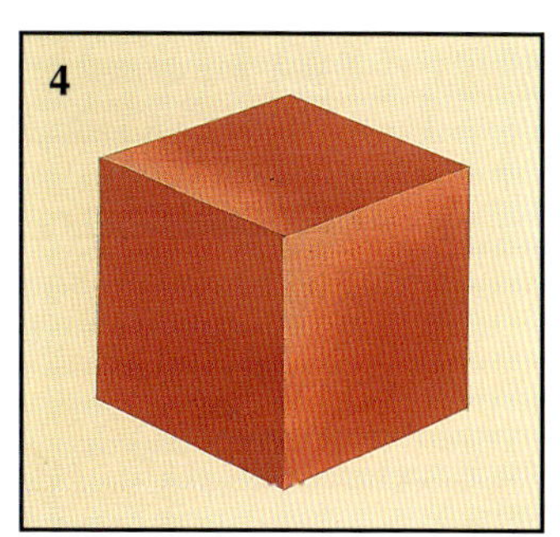

Being able to render these forms with an airbrush (on illustration board) helps in creating more advanced objects, such as an apple, orange, house, box, or fence post.

Cylinder

Step 1: Draw the cylinder. Lay stenciling film over the cylinder, and then make and number two cutouts.

Step 2: Remove the first cutout and spray at the top.

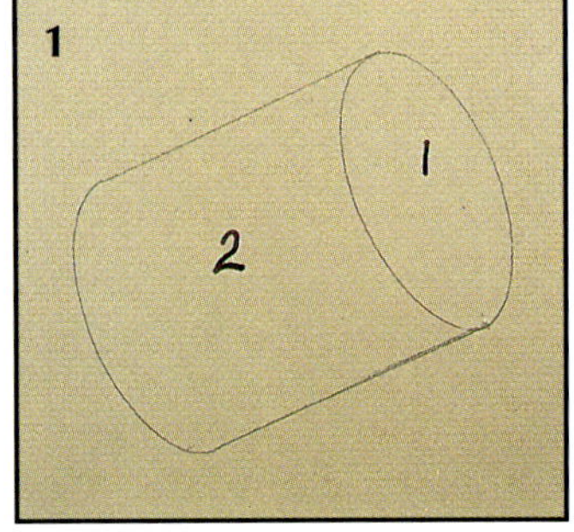

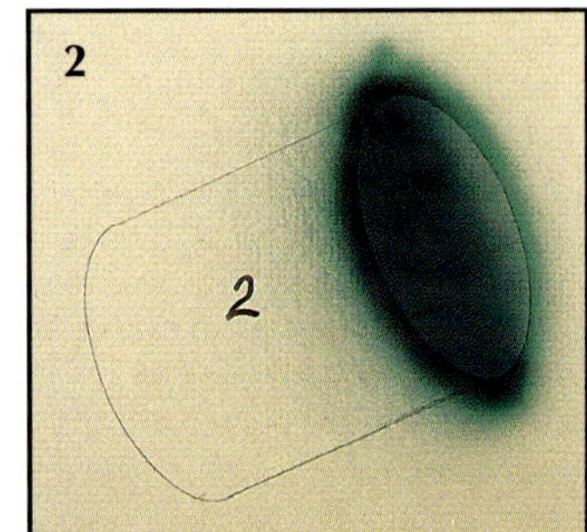

Step 3: Remove the second cutout and spray the side of the cylinder.

Step 4: Add white highlights on the side of the cylinder, and then remove the stencil.

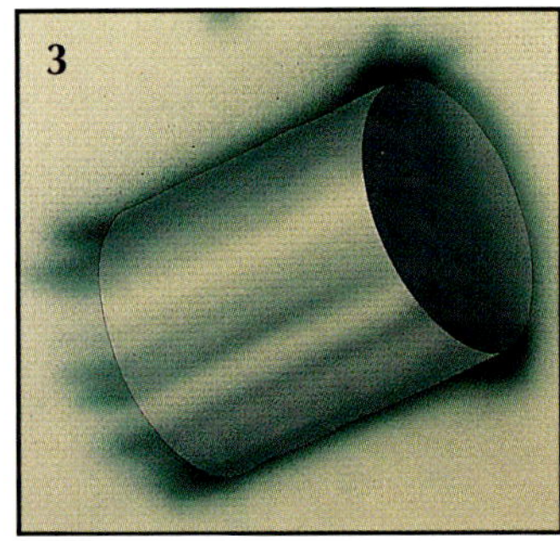

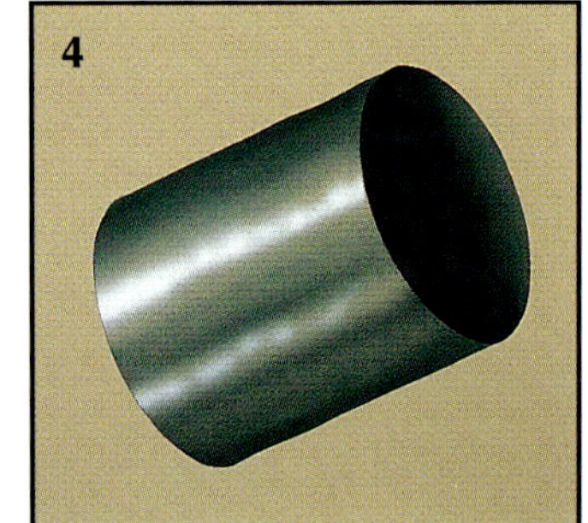

Cone

Step 1: Draw the cone. Place stenciling film over the board and make two cutouts on the cone.

Step 2: Remove the cutout at the bottom and spray that area. When dry, replace the stencil.

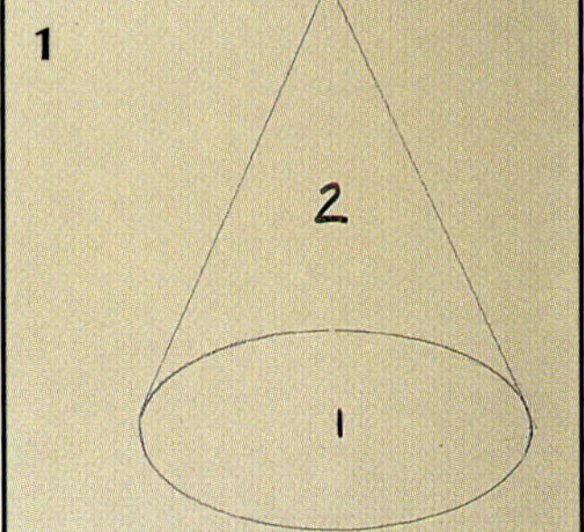

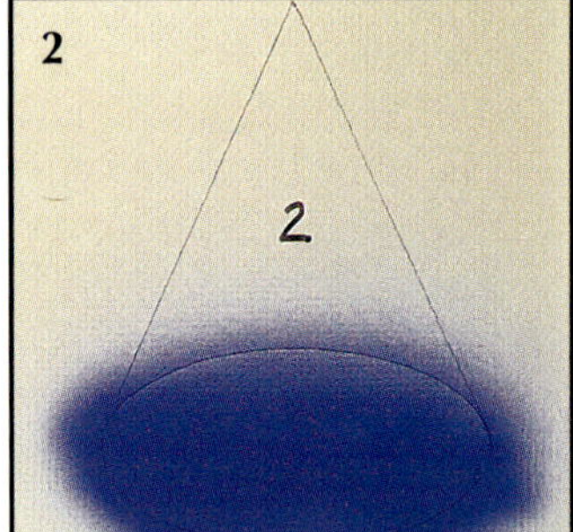

Step 3: Remove the stencil on the side and spray that area.

Step 4: Add white highlights to the side of the cone, and then remove the stenciling film.

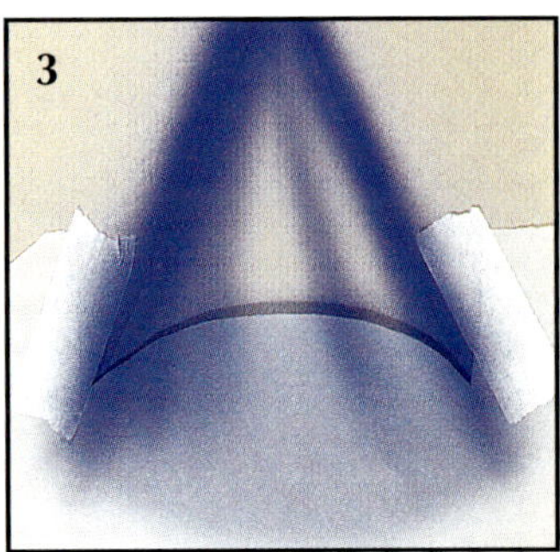

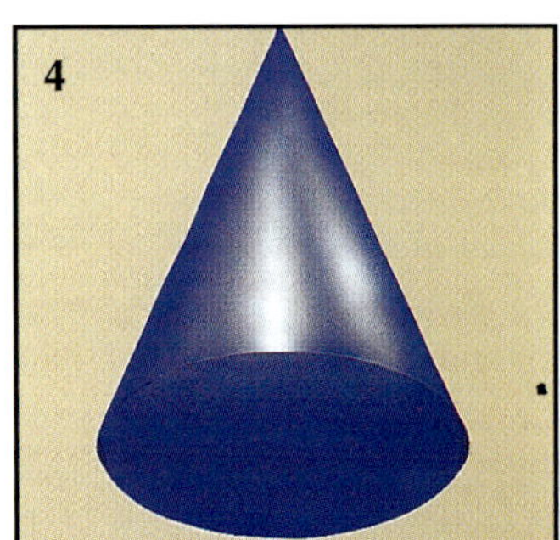

How to Paint Wallpaper with Cast Shadows

Step 1: Paint the background with yellow ochre and zinc white. At this point, it is pointless to draw the design of the wallpaper because it will be covered with gouache.

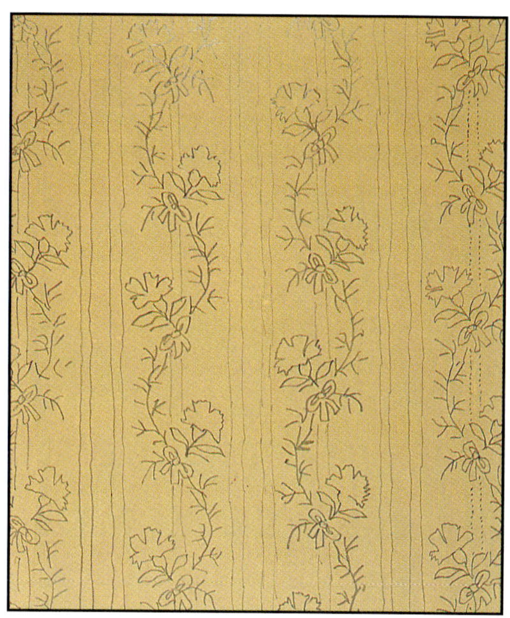

Step 2: Draw the design of the wallpaper over the background. You can use the slide projection method (see page 10) or create your own design.

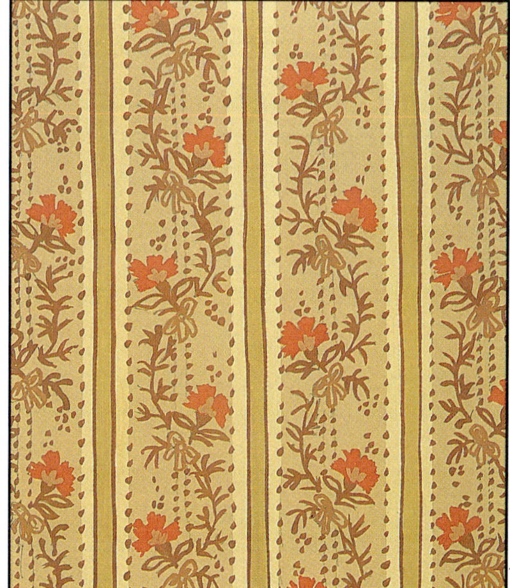

Step 3: Paint the pattern with the desired colors. Gouache is superb for making wallpaper in a painting, because it was once used for surface-pattern design work.

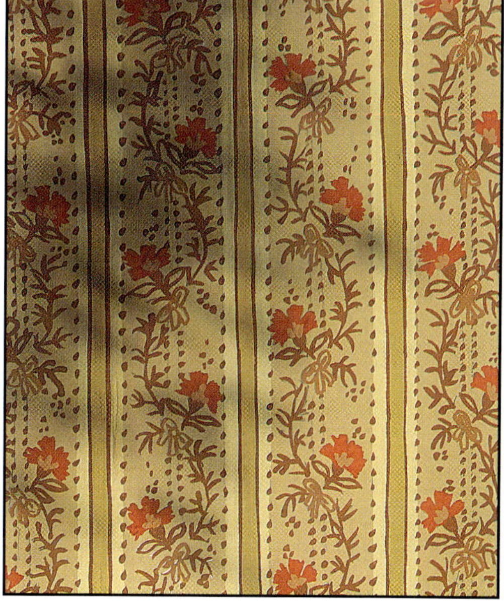

Step 4: Airbrush a light shadow of a plant over the design with black watercolor. Using watercolor instead of gouache allows the wallpaper to show through the shadow.

How to Paint Silver

Step 1: Establish the basic light and dark patterns by leaving the white of the board for the brightest highlights and applying dark gouache—alizarin crimson, burnt umber, and ivory black—in the background with a brush. The bowl is placed on top of a book, which is reflected in the silver.

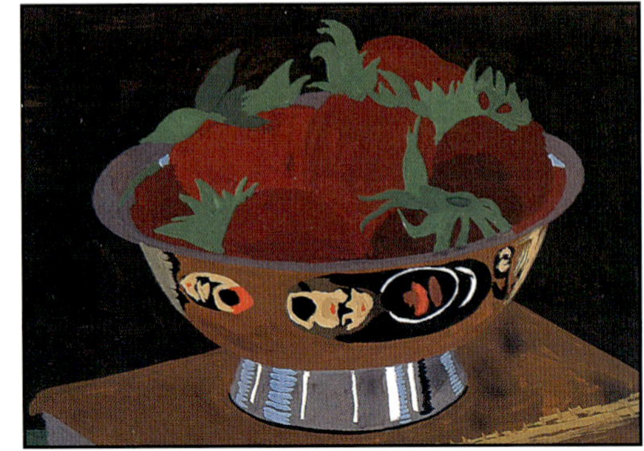

Step 2: Apply the middle tones and some lighter tones of burnt sienna and yellow ochre, cobalt blue and zinc white, burnt umber and zinc white. Define the strawberries with cadmium red light. Then lighten the book, leaves, and underside of the bowl with yellow ochre and permanent green light.

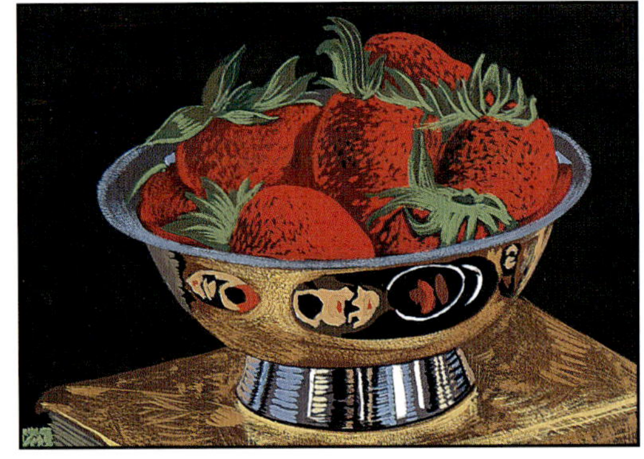

Step 3: Using ivory black watercolor, airbrush shadows on the strawberries and on the left and underside of the bowl. Note that the foreground objects are reflected in the silver bowl.

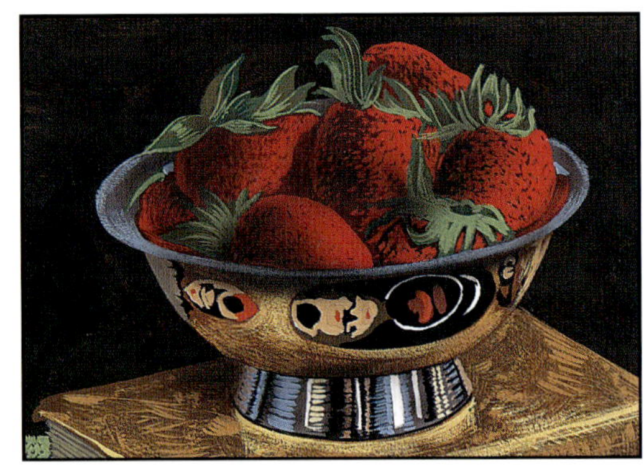

Step 4: Airbrush white highlights onto the silver bowl. Then paint the highlights on the strawberries with a #1 brush using titanium white gouache.

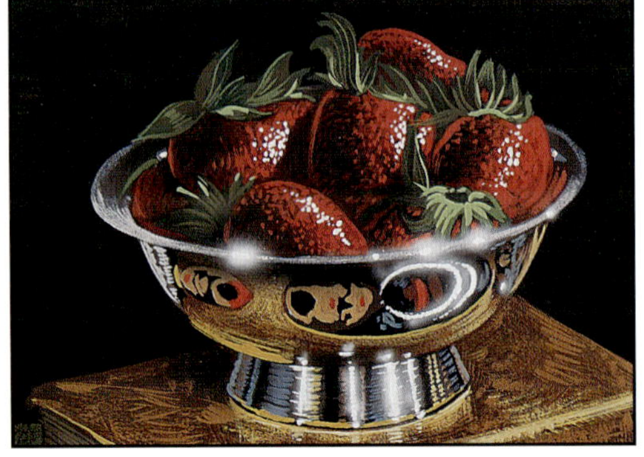

How to Paint an Apple and a Strawberry

Step 1: The first step in any painting is to complete the underpainting. Paint the apple and strawberry with their local colors—the strawberry is straight cadmium red, the apple is yellow ochre and some permanent green light in areas of the apples. The lighter areas of the apple are cadmium yellow mixed with zinc white. (These colors will be lightened as the painting progresses.)

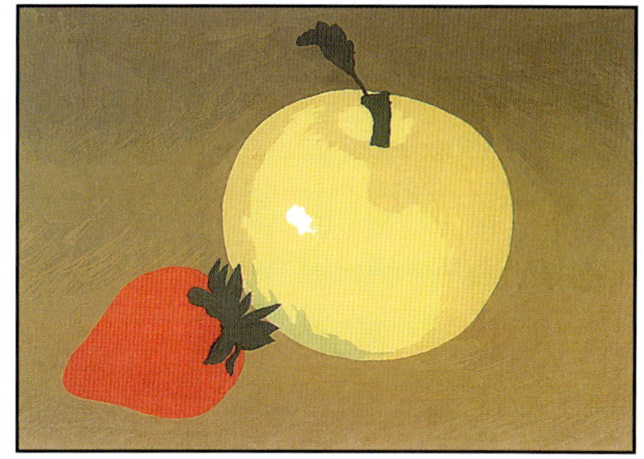

Step 2: Isolate the apple with a stencil. Airbrush the red patches with cadmium red gouache and then the shadows with black watercolor.

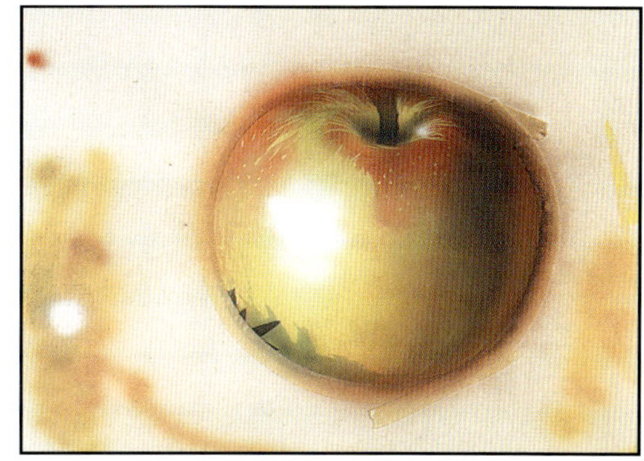

Step 3: Apply the shadows on the strawberry and the cast shadows from the fruit with the airbrush and ivory black watercolor. Then remove the stencil and use a strong, directional lighting from the left to create a three-dimensional feeling. Airbrush black watercolor over the shaded areas.

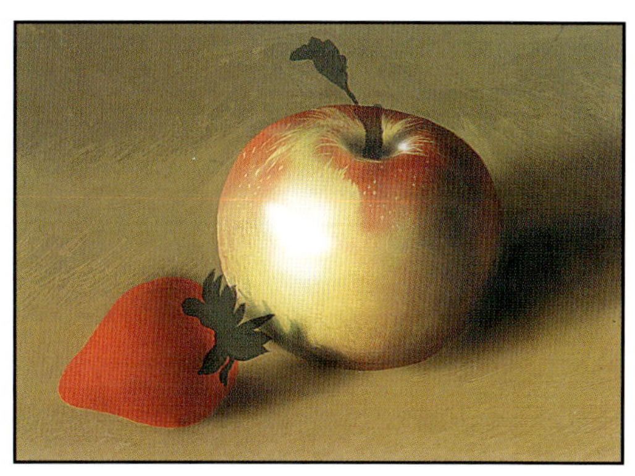

Step 4: Establish the highlights and add finishing touches. Add a stem to the apple with ivory black, permanent green, light yellow ochre, and zinc white. Then define the seeds on the strawberry with yellow ochre and ivory black. Apply pure titanium white to the centers of each highlight to make them as white as possible.

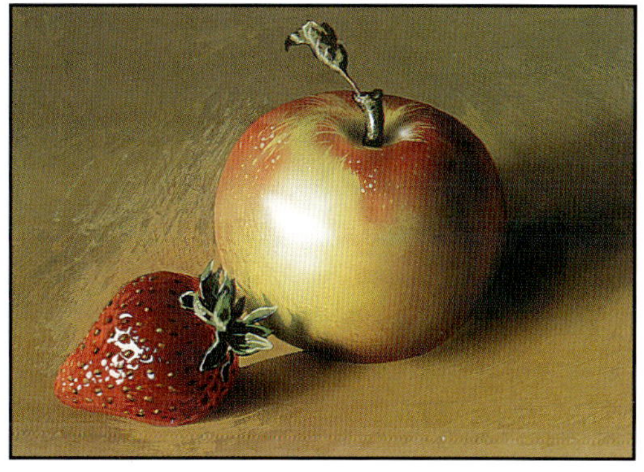

How to Paint a Persian Rug

Step 1: With an HB pencil, sketch the drawing on illustration board. Be sure to make the design accurate and complete. With photorealist paintings, the key to an exact likeness is to observe the small details, such as subtle shading, textures, details, and surfaces.

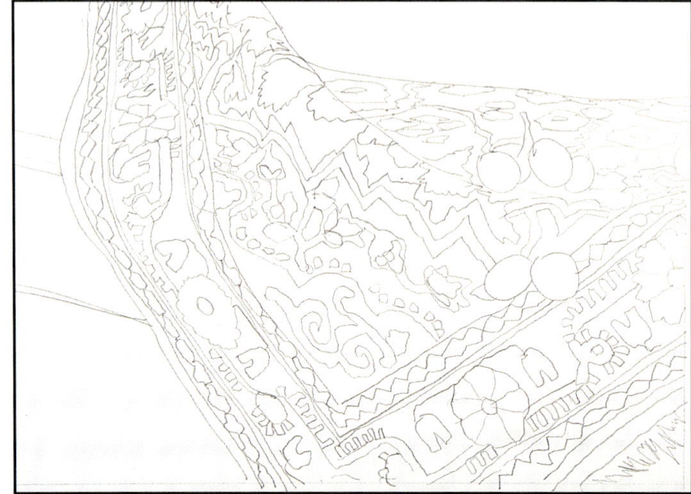

Step 2: Complete the underpainting with dark colors. Paint the colors of the rug in the same chroma as in the final painting but much darker in key. This way, light reds can be applied over darker reds, lighter blues over dark blues, and light yellows over darker yellows, allowing the darks to show through and creating an interesting rug texture.

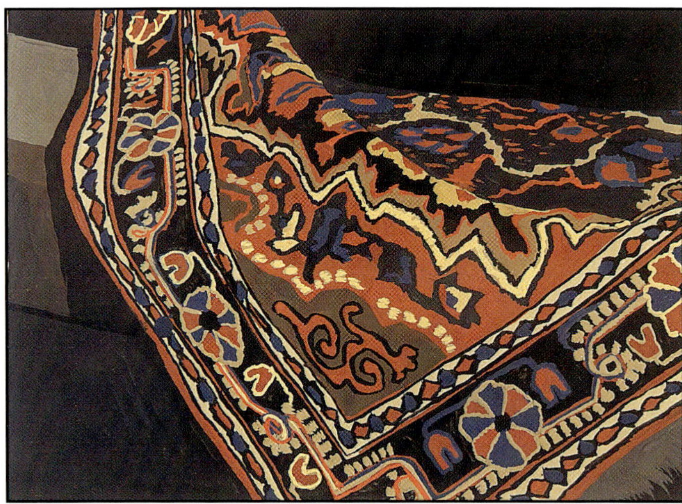

Step 3: When the underpainting is dry, paint over the same area to establish the medium tones (local colors) of the rug. Apply these tones with a small watercolor brush in hundreds of stippled dots. The paint is a creamy consistency—not too thin or too thick. Gouache is excellent in painting light colors over dark colors because of its inherent opacity.

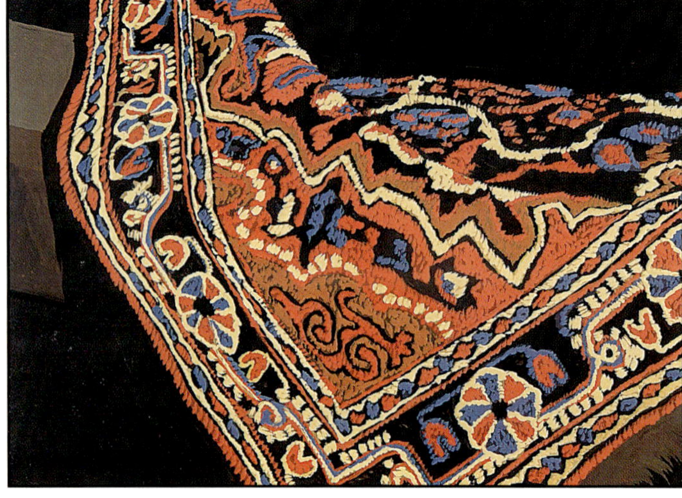

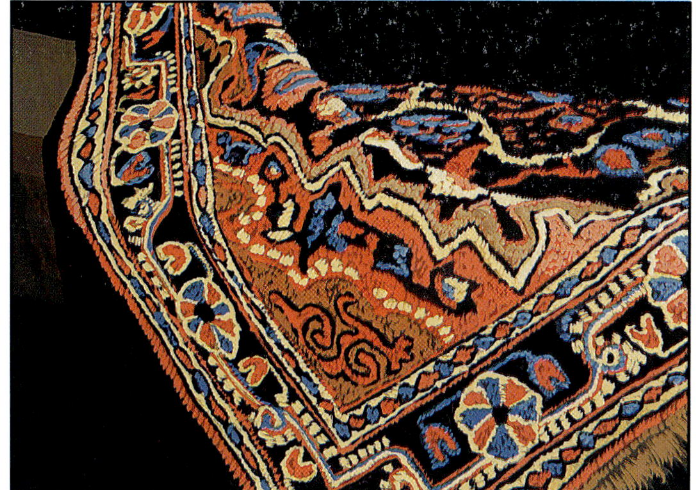

Step 4: When the middle tones are dry, apply the lighter tones to create a feeling of light falling on the rug. The light tones also help to create depth. Note: These are not the very lightest tones.

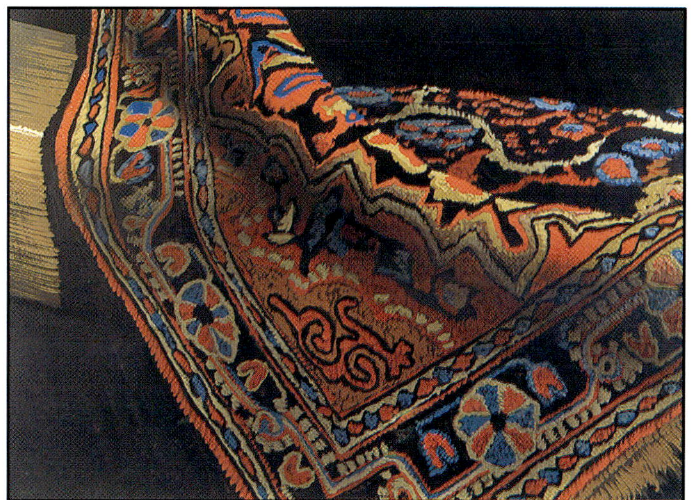

Step 5: Airbrush black watercolor onto the areas in shadow. Note: It is better to gradually build up the darks in several layers than to spray too quickly and create a glaze of watercolor that is too dark. The watercolor will soak into the gouache and slowly make it darker. Allow time for the paint to be absorbed before applying another layer—it may already be dark enough.

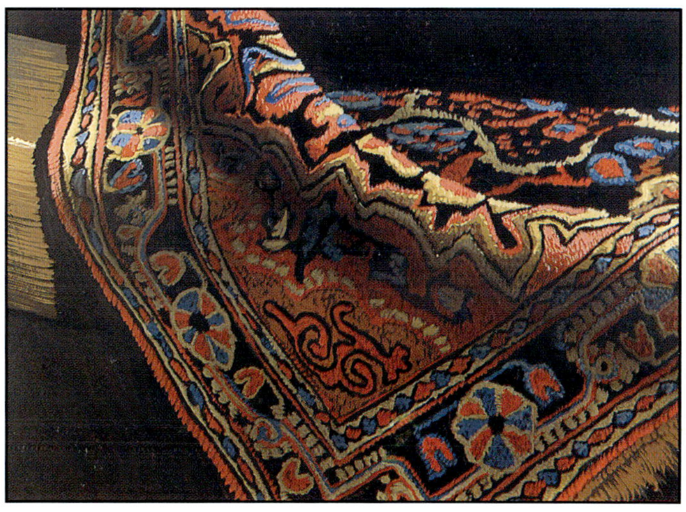

Step 6: The final step is the most relaxing and enjoyable. Place the lightest touches on the rug where the direct light hits. To complete the rug study, use a very small watercolor brush and the lightest tints of each color (e.g., pink on red, light blue on blue) to accent the tints along the ridges of the folds. This is the standard approach used for painting tapestry. Paint in a logical, sequential manner.

How to Paint Wood

Step 1: Painting wood is easy, because you can embellish it in many ways and it will still look natural. Lay down the solid tone of the basic wood color with yellow ochre and burnt sienna.

Step 2: Add the larger grain markings with a watercolor brush in a drybrush manner using yellow ochre mixed with burnt umber and ivory black.

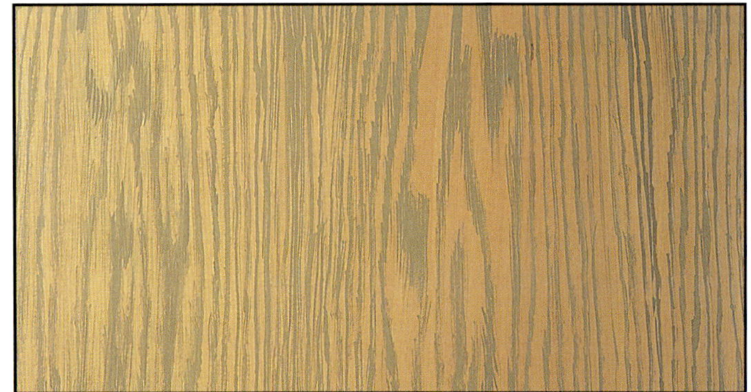

Step 3: When the wood grain is dry, establish some darker markings—as well as patina in the wood, holes, grain lines, and textures on the surface of the wood—with a mix of burnt umber, black, and a touch of yellow ochre.

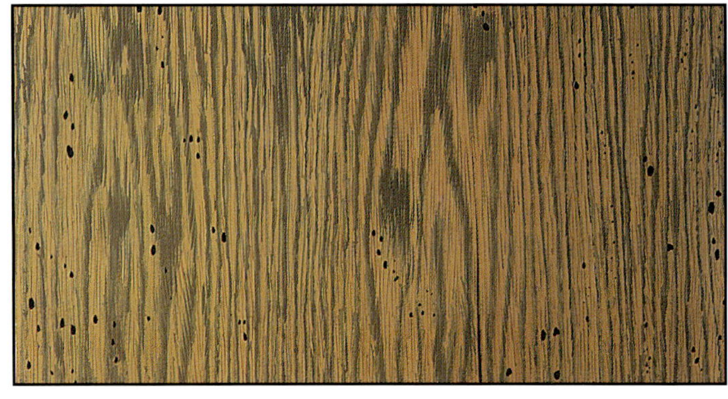

Step 4: Apply lighter tints to accent the wood and the edges of the hole. If the light is coming from the left, highlight the hole along the right of the rim—and vice versa. Tip: Study different types of wood to see the ways that they grow. Oak is different than pine, which is different than maple, and so forth.

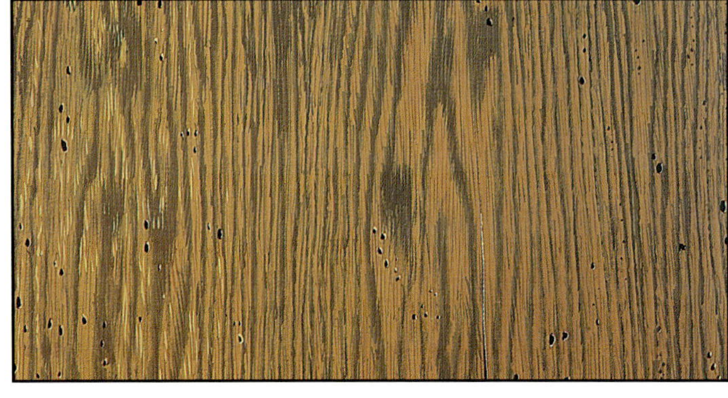

How to Paint Glass

Step 1: Here, seven different colored bottles are used to demonstrate the versatility of gouache. Paint the bottles darker than they actually are because they will be lightened later in the painting. Lay the underpainting with straight ivory black, grey-blues, and medium greys.

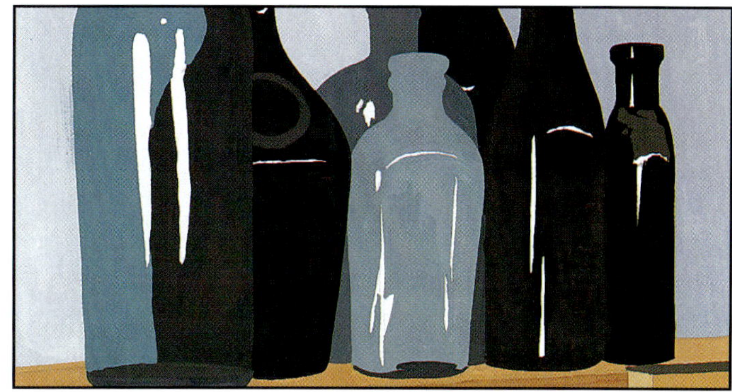

Step 2: Use middle tone colors to define the forms of the bottles. Leave some areas unpainted to serve as bright highlights and to help gauge the colors. Use the drybrush technique to create subtle blending of tones.

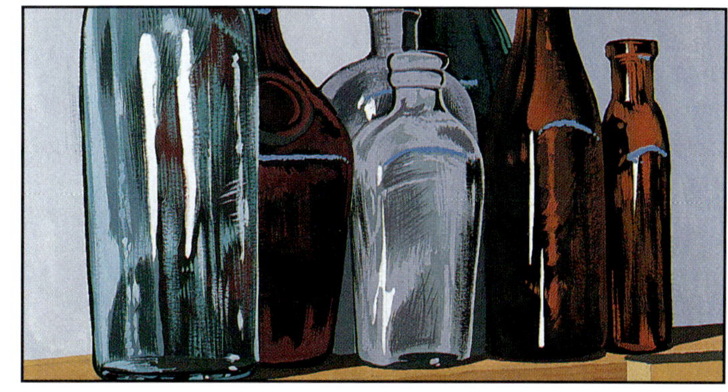

Step 3: Airbrush the shadows with ivory black watercolor. The shadows cast by the bottles help to create form, depth, and realism.

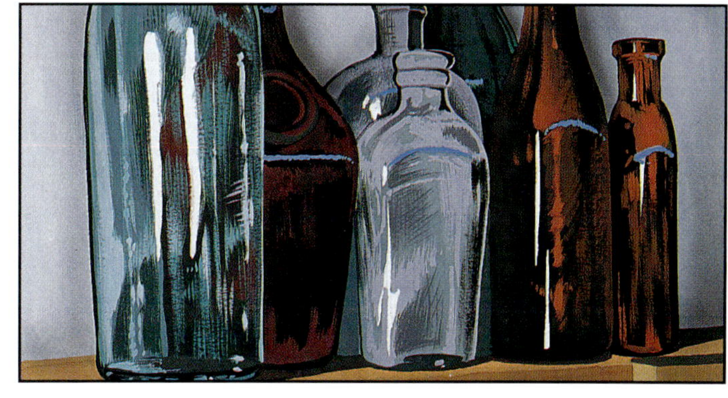

Step 4: Add highlights with pure titanium white gouache. The condition of the bottle determines the highlight. For example, an old, dusty bottle has soft, blurry highlights, and a new, clean bottle has well-defined, crisp highlights. The key to photorealism is to carefully study the differences between objects.

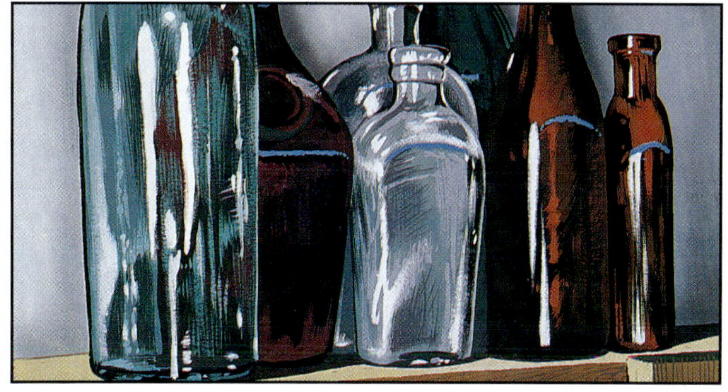

How to Paint Old Books

Step 1: This setup demonstrates how gouache can be used to make extremely fine, opaque lines to create the look of worn pages, threadbare bindings, and scuffed surfaces. Paint in the dark values with a brush using ivory black (bottom book), burnt umber and ivory black (top book), and yellow ochre mixed with burnt umber (middle book).

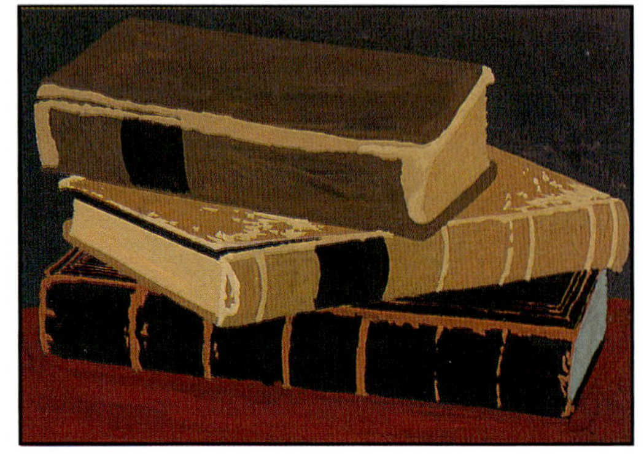

Step 2: When the dark values are dry, lighten the colors with the same colors as the underpainting tinted with zinc white. Use a brush and yellow ochre and zinc white to create the textures on the spines of the books. Stipple the foreground carpet with cadmium red mixed with zinc white.

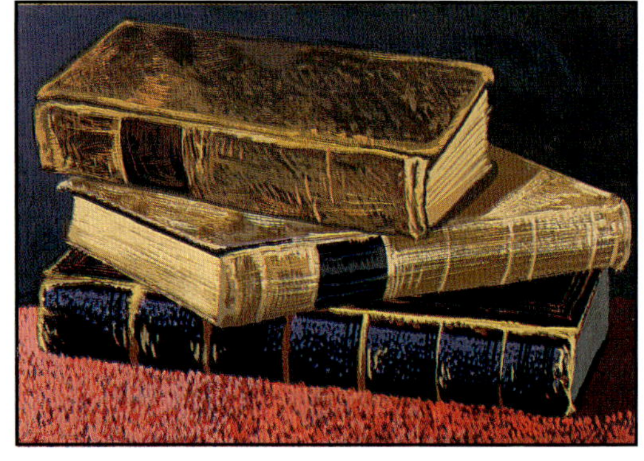

Step 3: Use the airbrush to spray shadows of ivory black watercolor on the books. To ensure spray doesn't fall on unwanted areas, place paper over the books as a stencil.

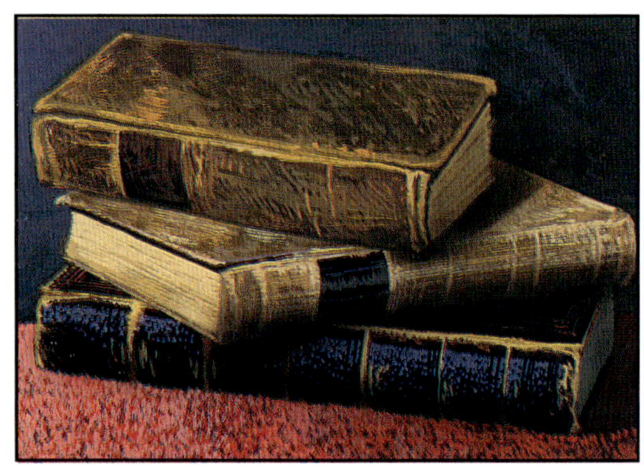

Step 4: Highlight the worn bindings using a small watercolor brush and touches of pure titanium white gouache. The pure white highlights add sparkle to the completed still life. Again, notice the technique of working from dark to light, applying highlights last.

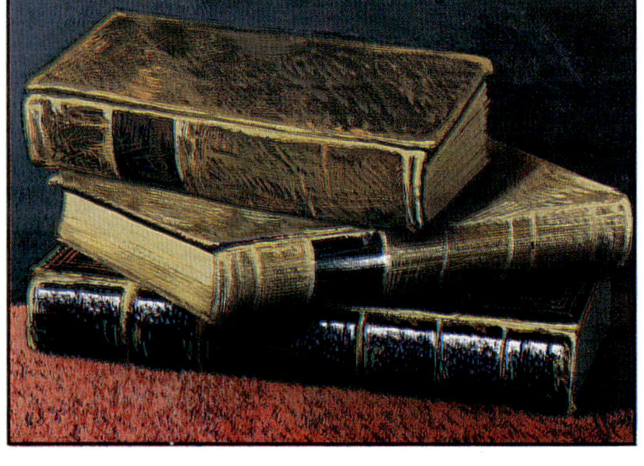

Soft-Edged Shadows

The closer a shadow is to the wall or surface on which it falls, the more defined the shadow will be. Try this experiment: Put your hand on a table with a light source overhead and slowly lift your hand. Notice how the shadow gets softer, larger, and blurrier as your hand moves toward the light. The shadow gets lighter until it eventually disappears. Remember this observation when creating shadow patterns in your paintings.

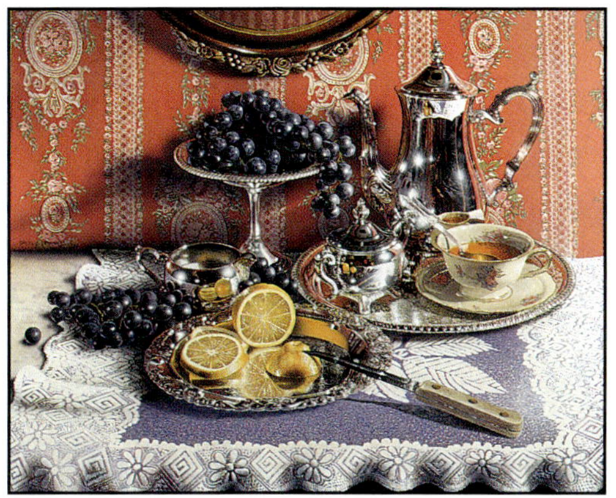

Note the soft, elongated shadows cast from the silver compote. The light is coming from the right, creating a cast shadow on the wall. Remember that shadows are always directly opposite the light source. Consistent shadows will add credibility to your work. Use the airbrush to render soft cast shadows.

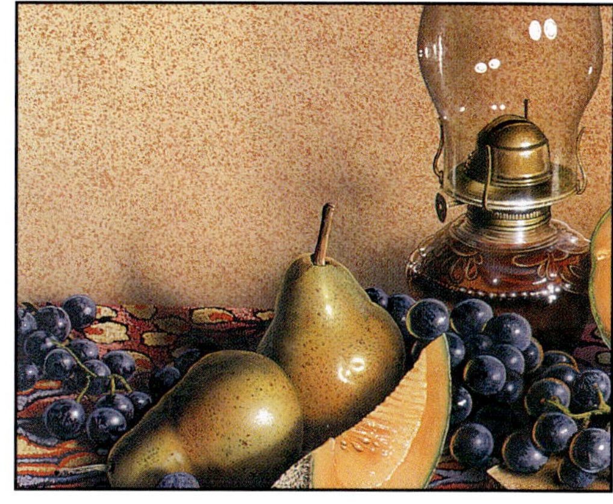

Because glass is transparent, it barely casts a shadow. In this detail, notice the interesting shadows from the fruit as they fall on the back wall. This soft, out-of-focus airbrushed effect adds a sense of depth to the painting because it effectively simulates real shadows.

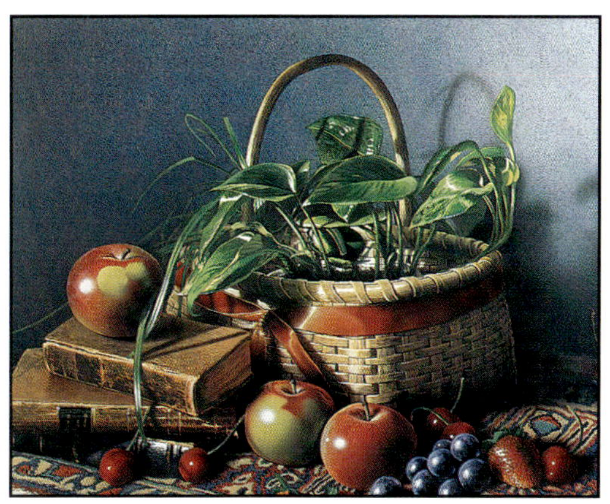

Shadows cast from the basket create a sense of mystery as the objects recede. The shadows also help differentiate the objects from the background wall. Note that they are at a distance from the wall, adding a greater sense of depth to the overall composition.

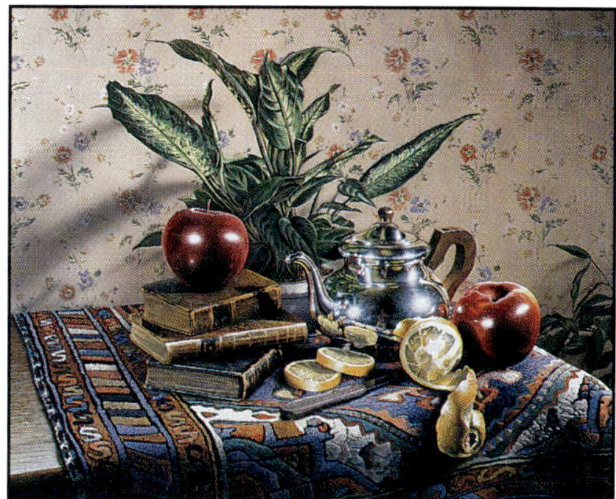

This is a dramatic example of soft-edged shadows cast on a background wall. The plant is struck by light from the right, creating a pattern of shadows on the left wall. The shadows help to add dimension, visual interest, space, and design to the area.

Shadows on Hard-Edged Objects

Shadows on hard-edged objects provide the opposite effect of soft-edged shadows (both often occur in the same painting). You can add a sense of drama to any painting by casting shadows on hard edges along with soft-cast shadows. Below are some examples of hard edges with shadows on them.

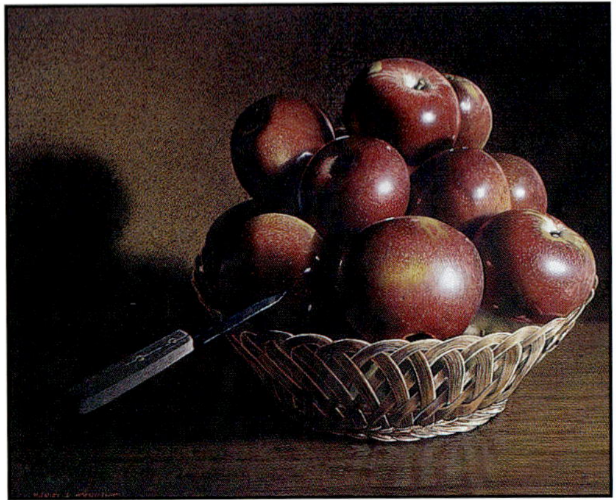

In this simple study of apples in a basket, the apples are painted with a hard edge, which reinforces the feel of their slick, shiny skin. Each apple had a separate stencil. The hard edges are achieved by airbrushing the shadows on the left of each piece of fruit.

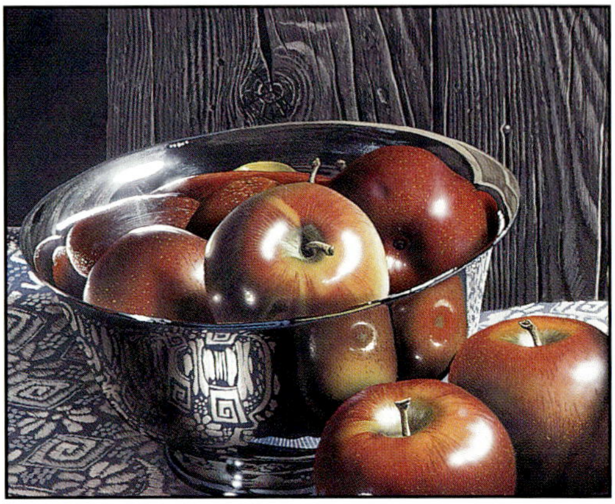

Again, the apples are painted with crisp, hard-edged shadows. Not only does the hard edge define the object itself, but also it contributes to the drama of contrast. A painting with both hard and soft edges has a more dramatic effect than one with only hard edges.

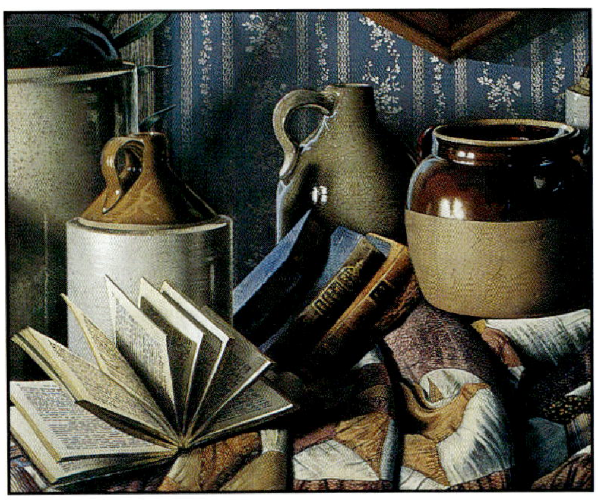

Crocks bathed in a dramatic, raking light have a hard edge on their right side. Also note that many objects have a subtle highlight in the shadowed edge, which is a result of reflected light. A piece of fruit can be totally dark on the shaded side, yet, along the edge, there is a lighter reflection.

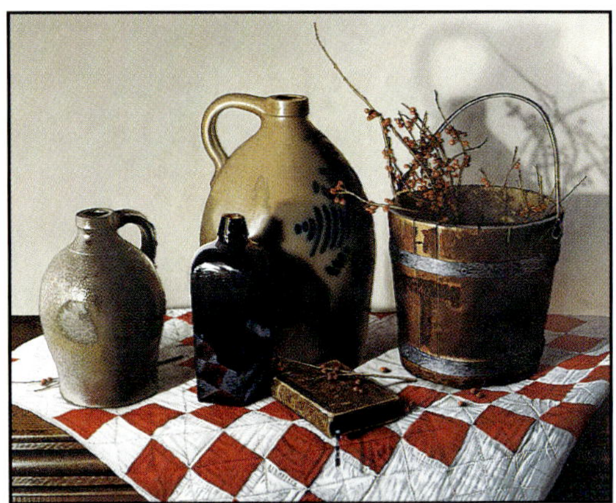

In high-contrast lighting, the hard edges of the crocks are rendered with an airbrush and black watercolor. The watercolor glaze allows you to see details within the shadows. Use stencils to create hard-edged shadows. A free-hand attempt would make the edges soft and misty.

Highlights

Although the term "highlight" implies a pure white sparkle, a highlight can also be the brightest area. In this painting, the lightest areas (apart from the white on the far pear) are the lightest yellows on the petals of the daisy. There are instances in painting when the brightest spots will simply be tints of the colors of the object. Too many pure white highlights can be distracting.

There are times, however, when the purest white available will make the highlights "shout" with importance. Here, the highlights on the ceramic are hard and bold, creating the feeling of hard, baked ceramic that is shiny.

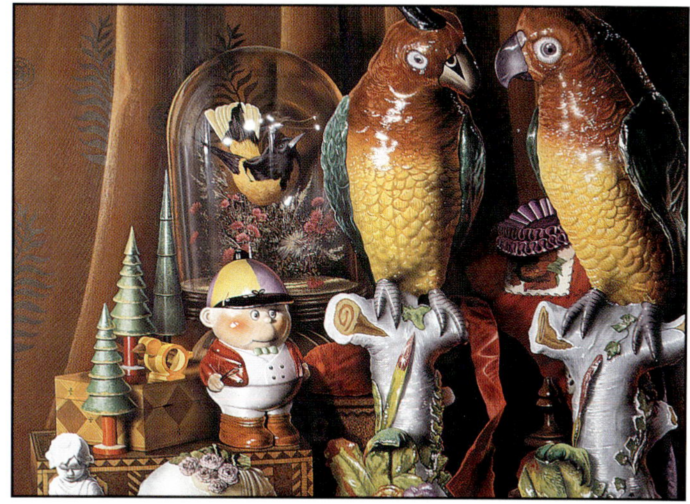

At other times, highlights will be diffused, soft, and glowing. With the airbrush, the highlights on the apples are sprayed on with titanium white to create the soft glow of the floodlights on the smooth skins. After the initial highlights are applied, the very center of each glow is highlighted with a small brush and pure titanium white.

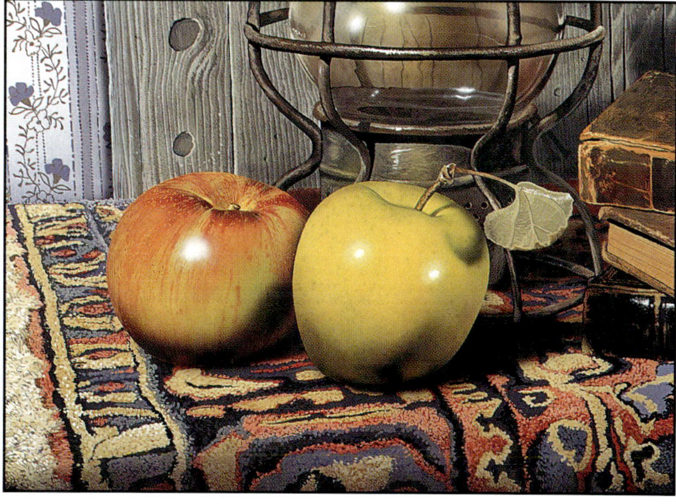

Demonstration: *August Afternoon*

Step 1: Draw the subject on 30" x 40" illustration board with an HB pencil (an HB makes a dark line that does not smear). Lightly indicate the background trees and work out the details of the young girl. With an airbrush, spray a mixture of cerulean blue, Naples yellow, and zinc white (all gouache) in the sky to achieve an atmospheric effect. Airbrush the reflection of the sky in the water with cerulean blue, zinc white, and cobalt blue.

Step 2: Paint the elements from back to front—that is, paint the objects farthest away first. Paint the background stand of tall pines with viridian green and black gouache to create a deep, cool color. Over this, use a brush to highlight the areas in the trees that are backlit by the sun.

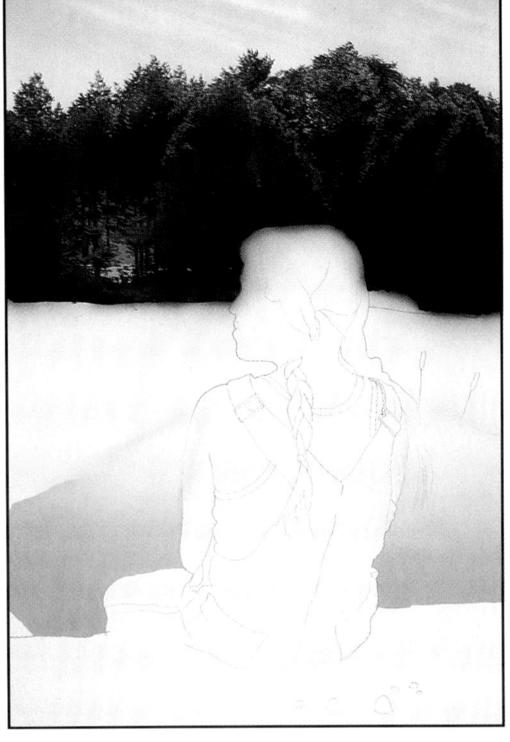

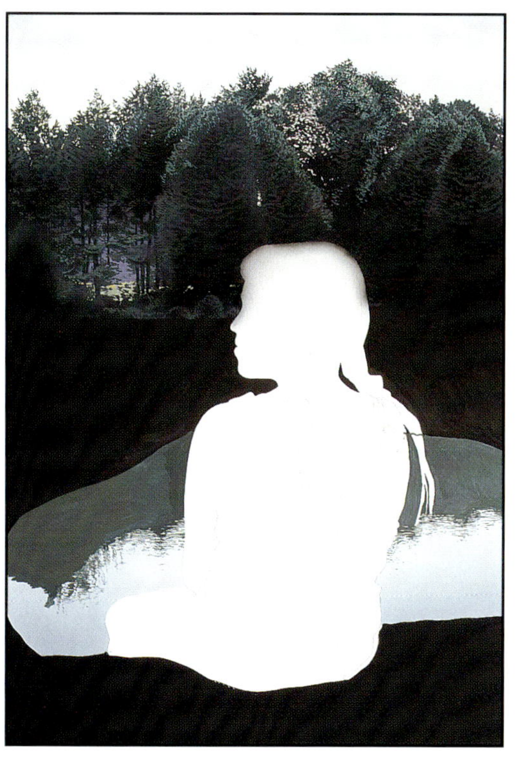

Step 3: Then paint the middle ground—an overgrown meadow lush with goldenrods, brown-eyed Susans, and grasses—with very dark colors of viridian and ivory black. Then add the reflections of the trees in the stream with a mixture of viridian, cerulean blue, ivory black, and white. Remember: With gouache, it is best to paint from dark to light.

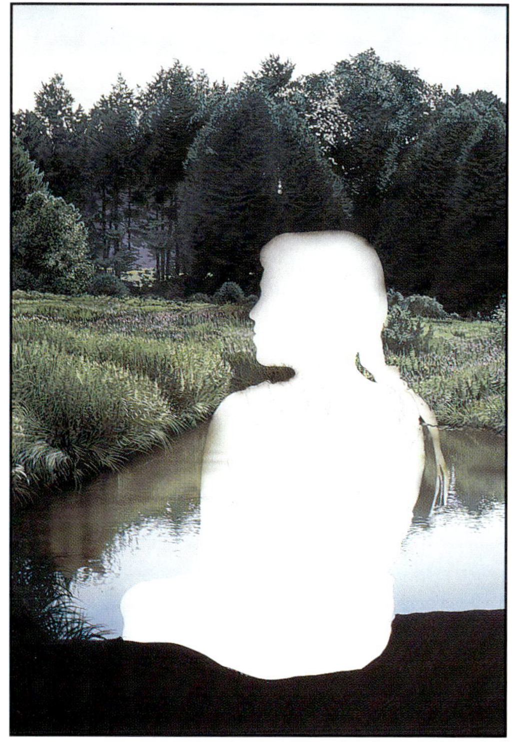

Step 4: Add highlights of zinc white mixed with cerulean blue and viridian to the background trees and paint the sky behind the trees. Paint the meadow with various shades of yellow ochre mixed with viridian, as well as whites, yellows, and lavenders. Intermittently, airbrush over the clumps of weeds in the meadow with transparent glazes of sap green and ivory black watercolor. Then establish the reflections in the water by painting a mixture of viridian, yellow ochre, and ivory black.

Step 5: Paint the foreground pebbles with a mixture of burnt umber, cobalt blue, and zinc white. Other pebbles can be ivory black, cobalt blue, and white. With the airbrush and transparent watercolors, paint the cast shadow from the girl. Then lay in the basic flesh tones and darken the hair. The flesh tones are cadmium red, white, and yellow ochre. The hair is burnt sienna and ivory black. Both have been painted in with a medium-sized watercolor brush (#4).

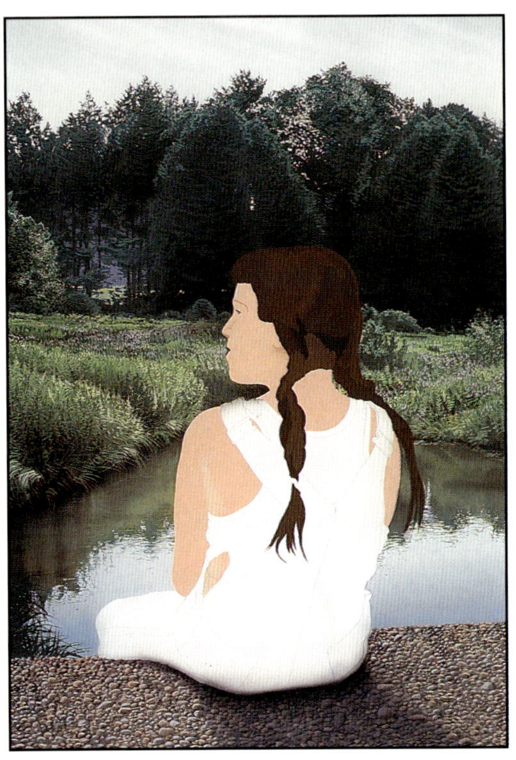

Step 6: Spend time painting the flesh tones to contrast with the highlights on the face and to create a backlit effect. Apply some pure white to the hair to gauge the values.

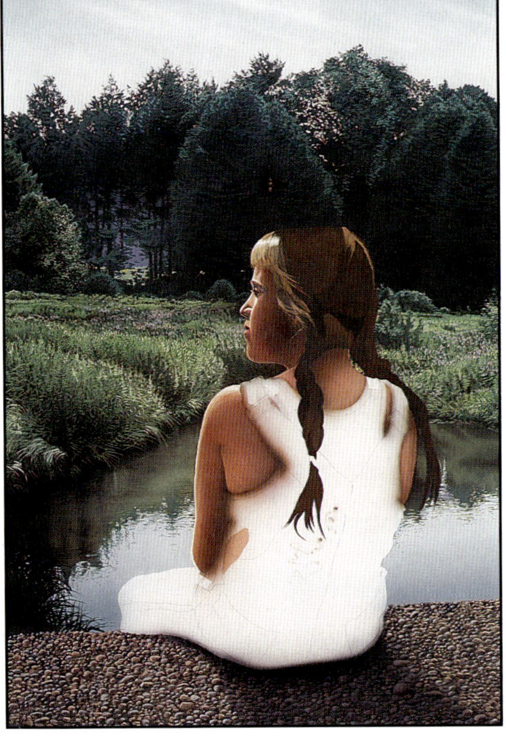

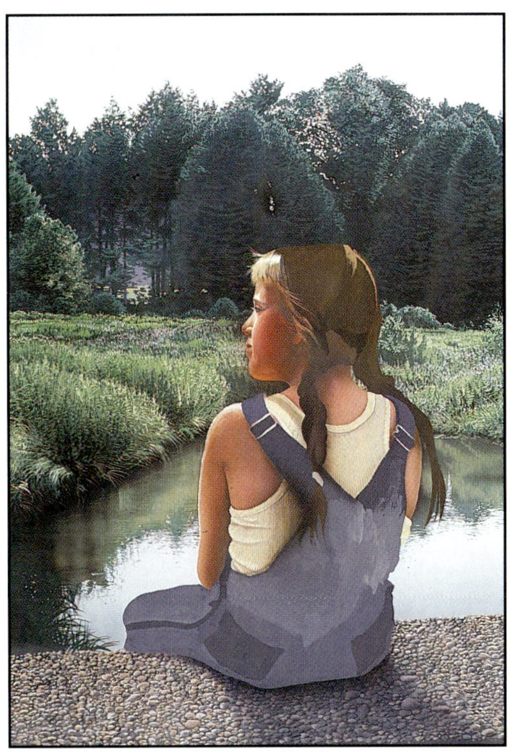

Step 7: Complete the tank top with Naples yellow, zinc white, and yellow. Using a small watercolor brush, create highlights with a lighter tint of the tank top color. Use a rigger to get the weave of the tank top. Then paint the overalls with cobalt blue mixed with ivory black and zinc white.

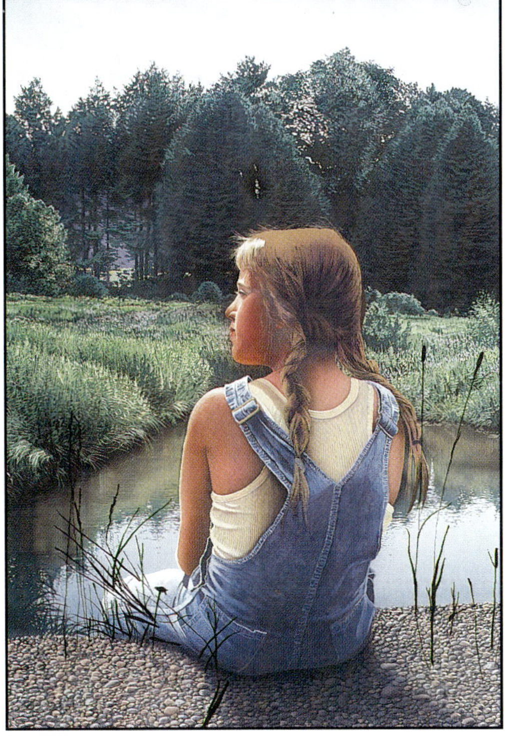

Step 8: After the overalls are painted, use the airbrush to place shadows on the lower part of the girl's body. Also indicate the grasses where she is sitting.

Step 9: Paint the silhouettes of the grasses in the foreground with straight ivory black. Use a rigger to underpaint the grass with viridian and black, and then highlight the grass with yellow ochre and white. Highlight the hair with a small watercolor brush using Naples yellow, zinc white, and yellow.

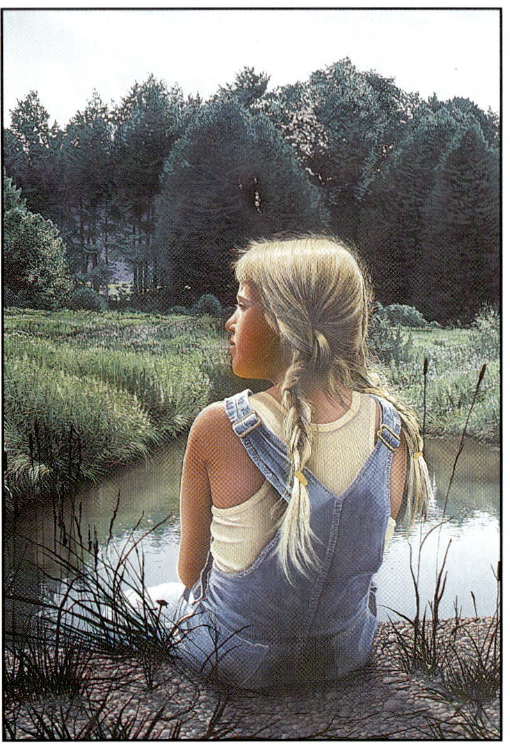

Step 10: After finishing the grasses, tone down the orange of the girl's face by airbrushing violet over the chin area. Then paint the barrettes. Finally, reestablish the pure whites so they appear bright and clean.

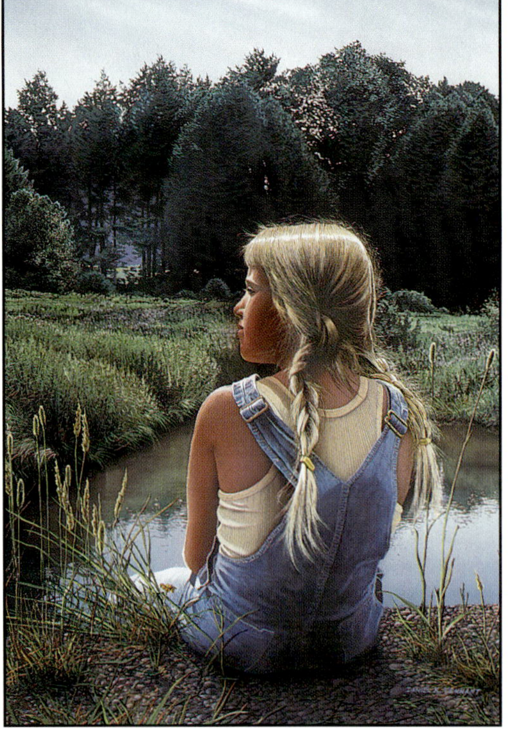

August Afternoon **(30" x 40") gouache on illustration board, collection of Anthony and Jane Balunas**

Planning a Painting

A logical, sequential method of painting eliminates guesswork. A painting is done in layers—with usually five layers maximum. Always start with the farthest layer, then the next closest, and so on, until you reach the closest layer.

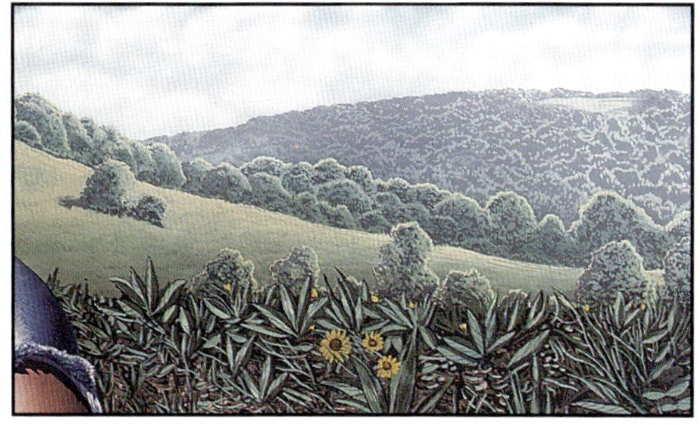

Background

The background is always painted first, whether it is a still life or landscape. The background establishes the depth of the painting and provides an underpainting over which closer objects are painted. Paint the background in layers—the sky, the farthest hill, the next closer hill, the trees over each hill, and then the field.

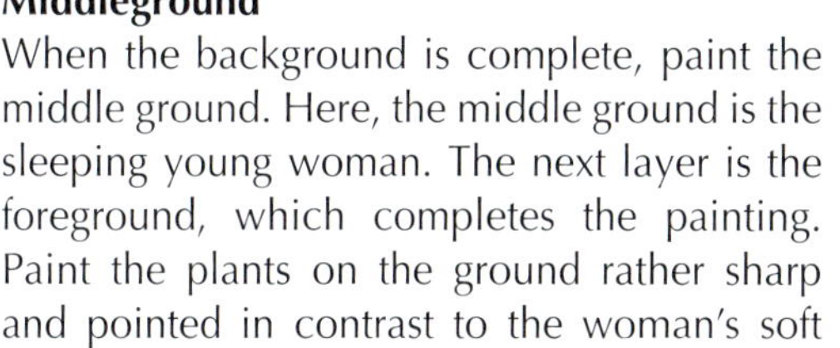

Middleground

When the background is complete, paint the middle ground. Here, the middle ground is the sleeping young woman. The next layer is the foreground, which completes the painting. Paint the plants on the ground rather sharp and pointed in contrast to the woman's soft skin and worn denim.

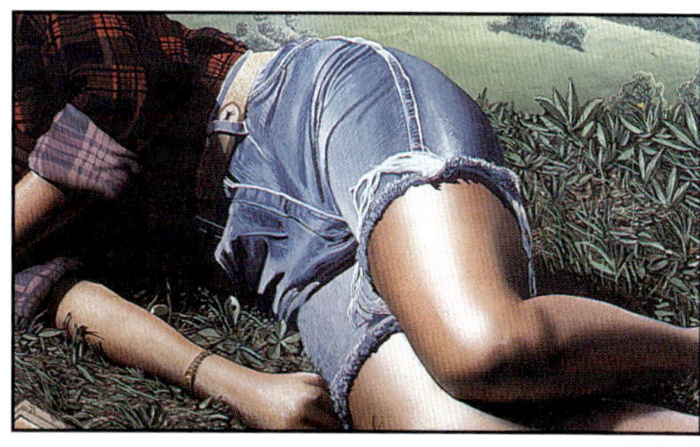

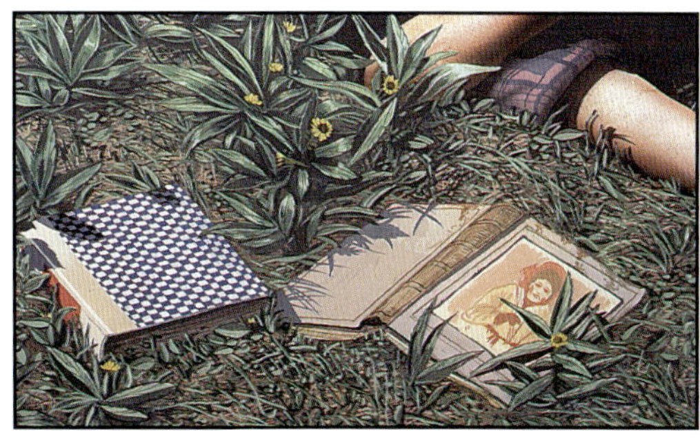

Foreground

The last step is always to add the final details in the foreground. Paint in the detailed books and finish the various plants that grow in front of and around the model. If you remember the painting order—(1) background, (2) middle ground, and (3) foreground—your level of success will increase with each painting.

This large figure painting was meant to symbolize summer. The rolling hills repeat the curvature of the body of the young woman who is asleep in the field.

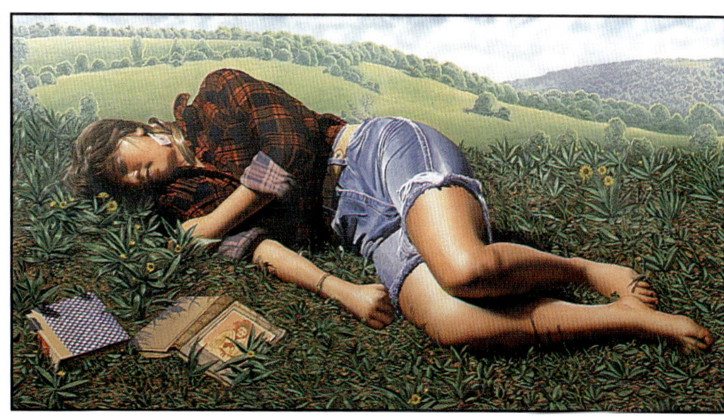

***Dreaming* (40" x 60") gouache on museum board, private collection**

Demonstration: *Still Life with Lantern*

Step 1: The most important aspect of a successful realistic painting is a strong drawing. Transfer the drawing to hot-pressed illustration board as explained on page 10.

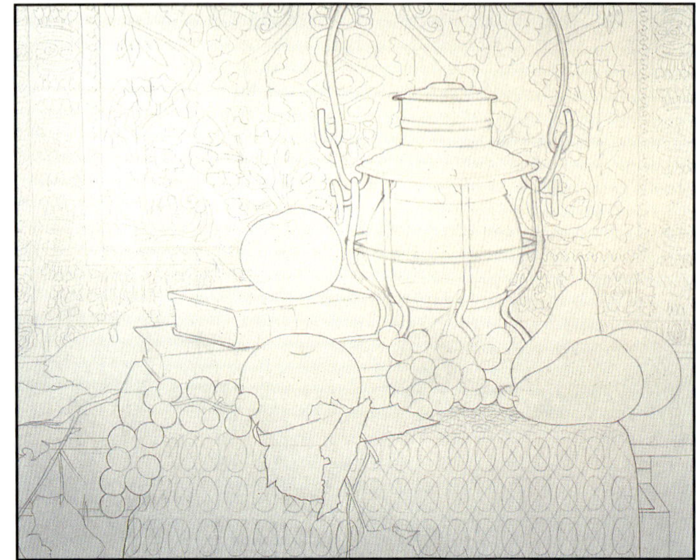

Step 2: Paint the background with thinned cerulean blue and cobalt blue gouache. Then complete the rug patterns with straight colors of cobalt blue, red, and yellow—all outlined with ivory black—using a small watercolor brush. Note that the rug is flat at this point—it has no shading or highlights. Because gouache is precise, it is being used in a linear manner in this painting.

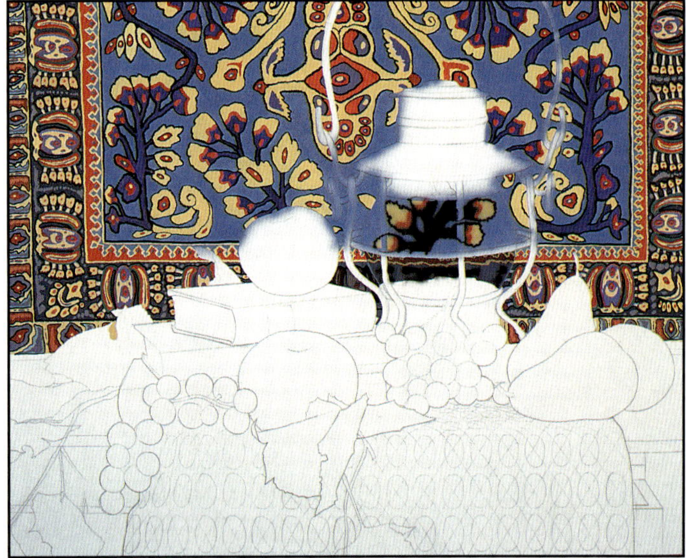

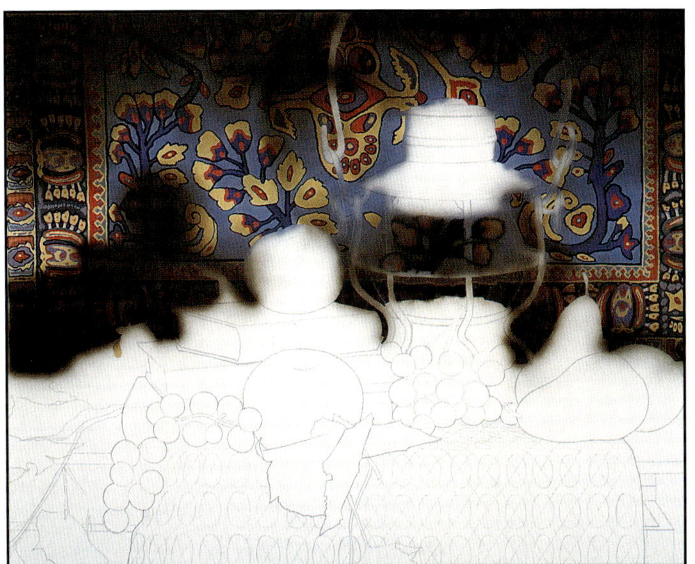

Step 3: Airbrush shadows in with a transparent watercolor mix of burnt umber and ivory black. Use watercolor so you can see the detail through the shadows. Shadows should tone down color, but they shouldn't destroy the detail.

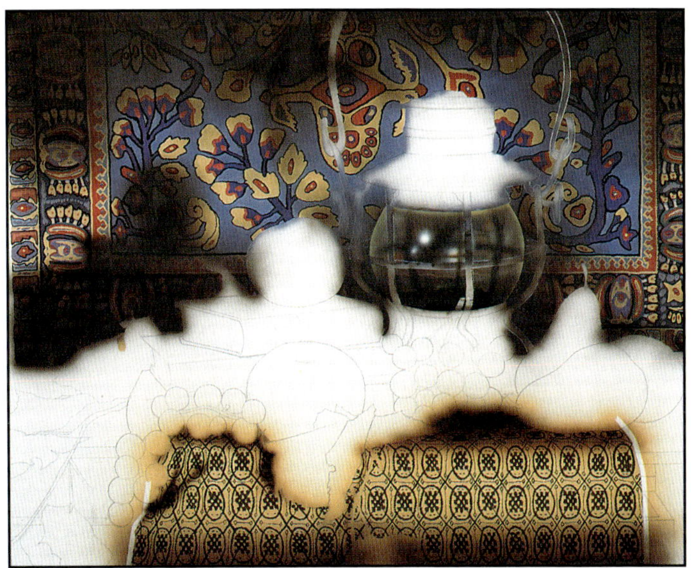

Step 4: Use ivory black, burnt umber, and yellow ochre gouache to airbrush over the globe of the lantern. Then mask off the globe (see step 7), and airbrush the foreground cloth with a base of Naples yellow gouache and a shade of burnt umber gouache. With a small watercolor brush, paint the pattern on the cloth with a mixture of burnt umber and ivory black gouache. Airbrush a cast shadow over the lower portion of the cloth using ivory black watercolor.

Step 5: Paint in the basic colors of each object—except for the apples and pears, which are untouched. These basic colors are darker than the objects will remain. Apply gouache with watercolor brushes.

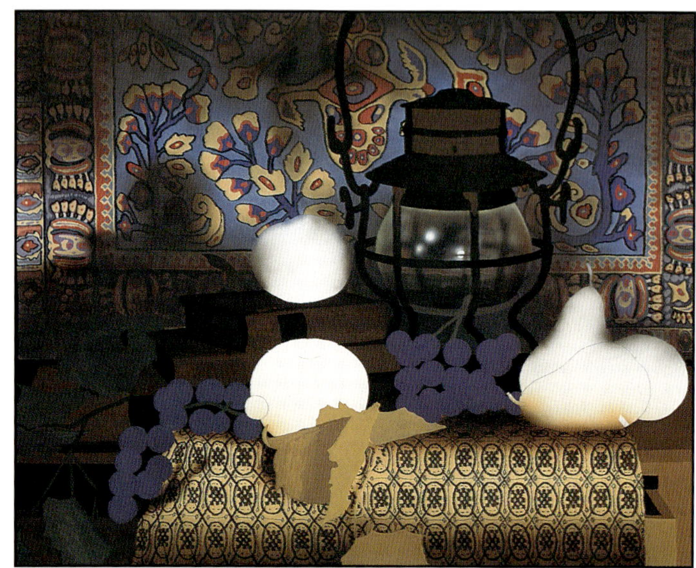

Step 6: Finish the books and lantern. Then airbrush black watercolor under the upper apple and behind the lower apple. Also airbrush the cast shadows from the pears, and then paint in the leaves and stems. Paint the highlights from the wood over the spattered patina and the lines of the wood grain. Airbrush the grapes to define their outlines. Also airbrush the shadows from the books and leaf shadows in the foreground.

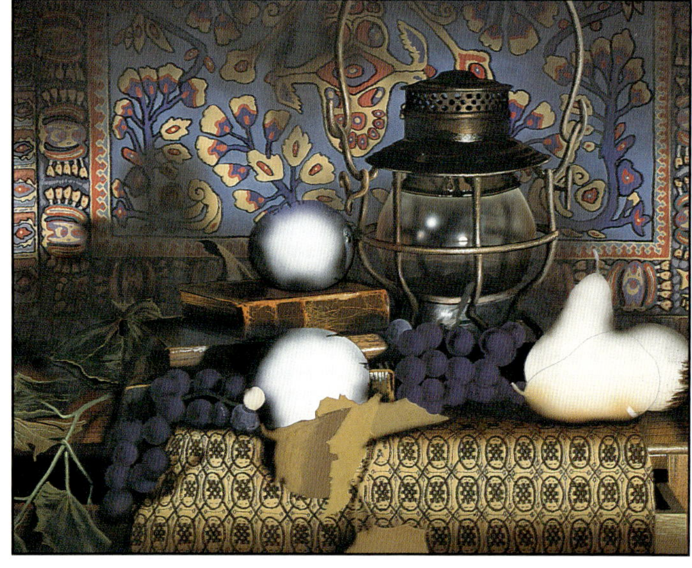

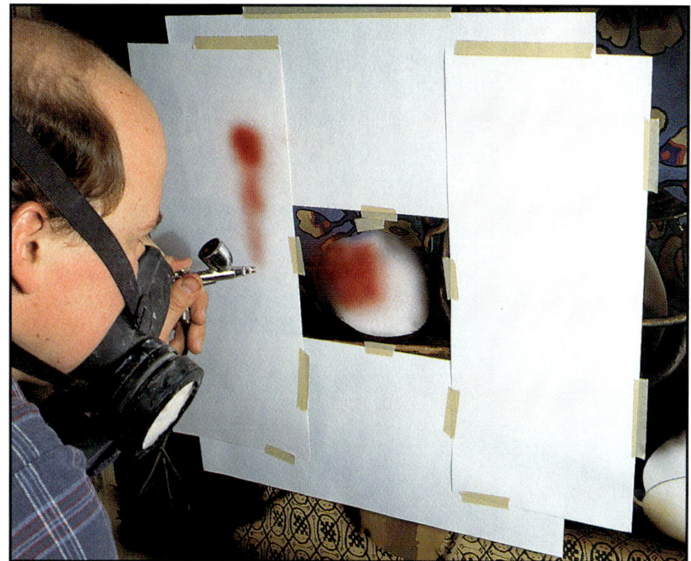

Step 7: When spraying with gouache, use stenciling film to isolate the fruit. Next, shade and then highlight the fruit. Then spray the apple with red gouache, and then spray the left side with ivory black gouache. Paint the speckles, stem, and highlights with a brush.

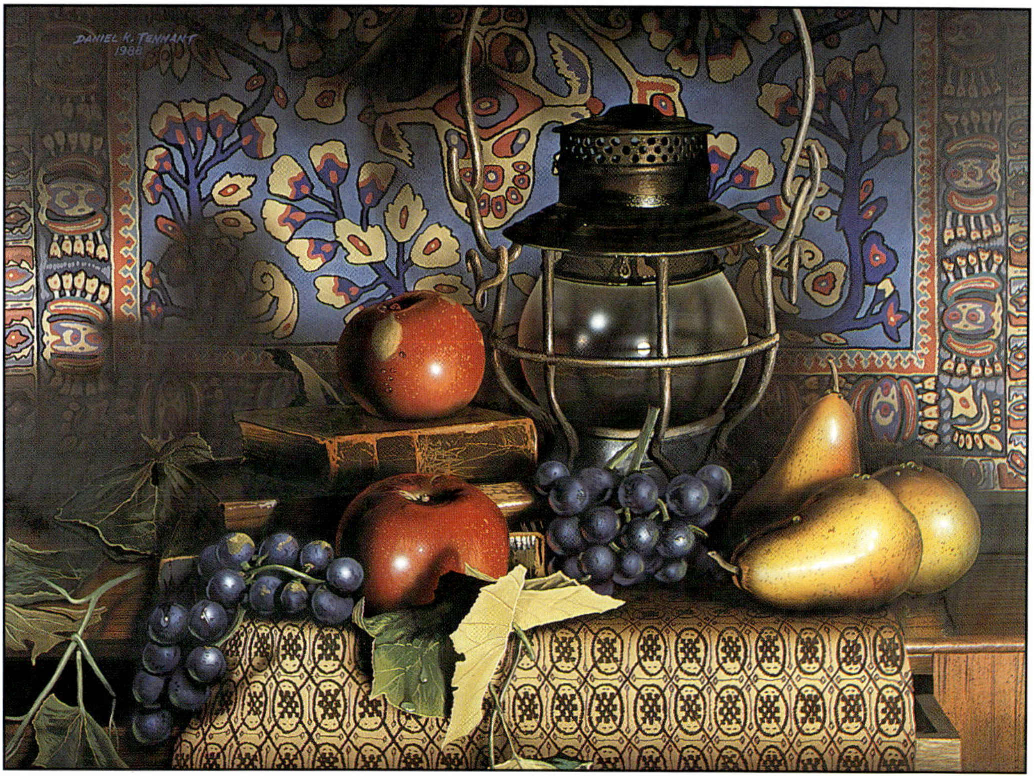

Still Life with Lantern **(27" x 36") gouache on illustration board, private collection**

Step 8: Finally paint in the pears, grapes, and foreground leaves—in that order. Remember: Always work from back to front. This saves a lot of touch-up work and provides a logical, sequential method of painting.

Demonstration: *Still Life with Satin Pillow*

Step 1: Use an HB pencil on hot-pressed illustration board to create the detailed drawing. Consider each part of the composition, so there will be no guesswork while painting. Next, paint the basic shapes of the pillow with a mixture of Naples yellow, zinc white, and alizarin crimson. Then airbrush in the folds and highlights with tints and shades of the same colors. Paint in some wrinkles with a rigger and scratch out some with a single-edge razor blade. Blacken a few sections of the Persian rug to gauge the colors. Cover the edges of the pillow with drafting tape to prevent the rug colors from bleeding.

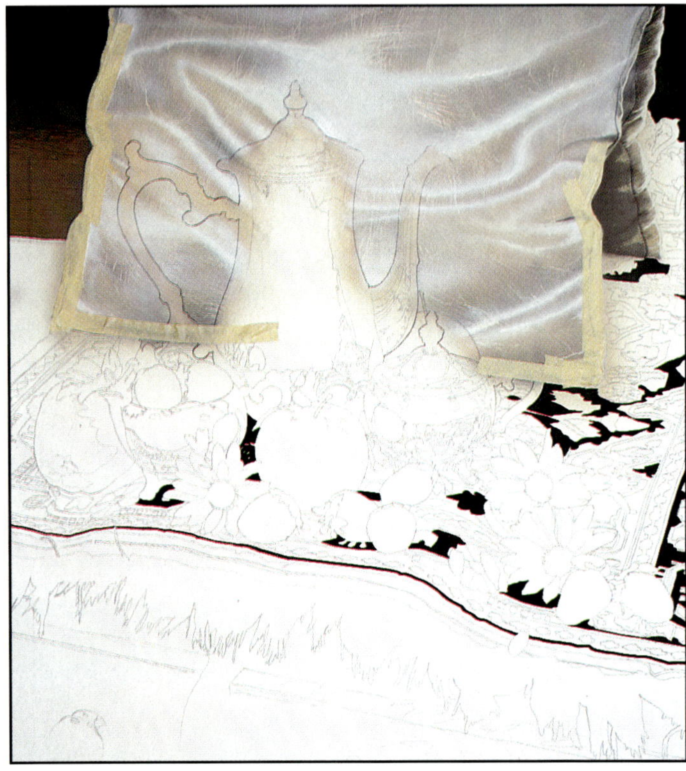

Step 2: Paint the Persian rug with basic colors: light cobalt blue, dusty pink, browns, and off whites. Outline areas with pure black. Use an airbrush for the cast shadows. Create texture by crosshatching over the entire rug with transparent watercolors (ultramarine blue and ivory black).

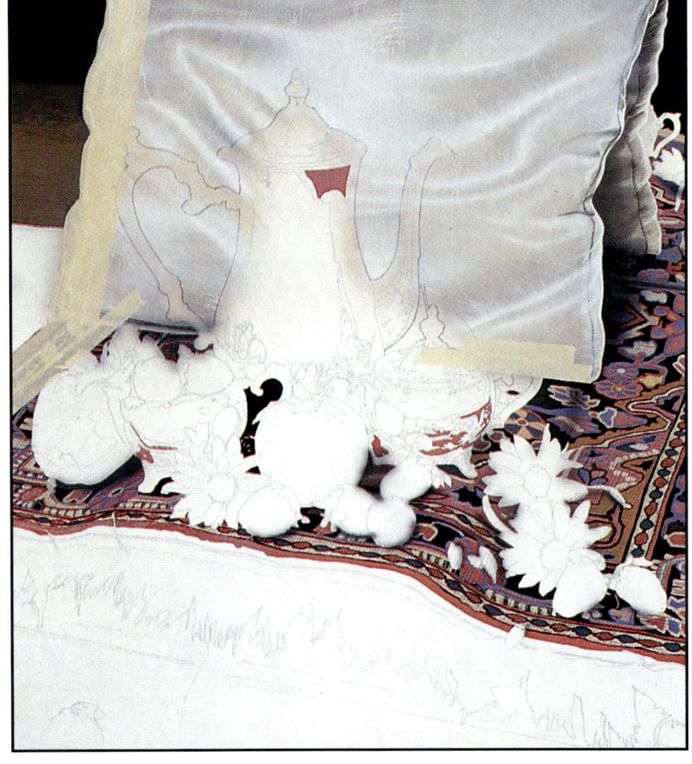

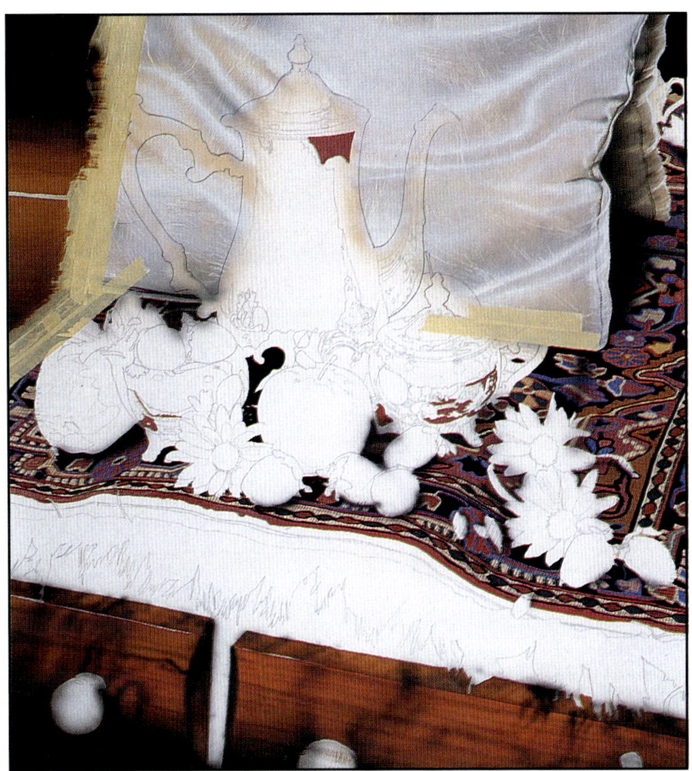

Step 3: Paint the foreground oak drawers with a mixture of yellow ochre, burnt sienna, and burnt umber. Use the airbrush to paint the basic patterns of the wood grain and the cast shadows.

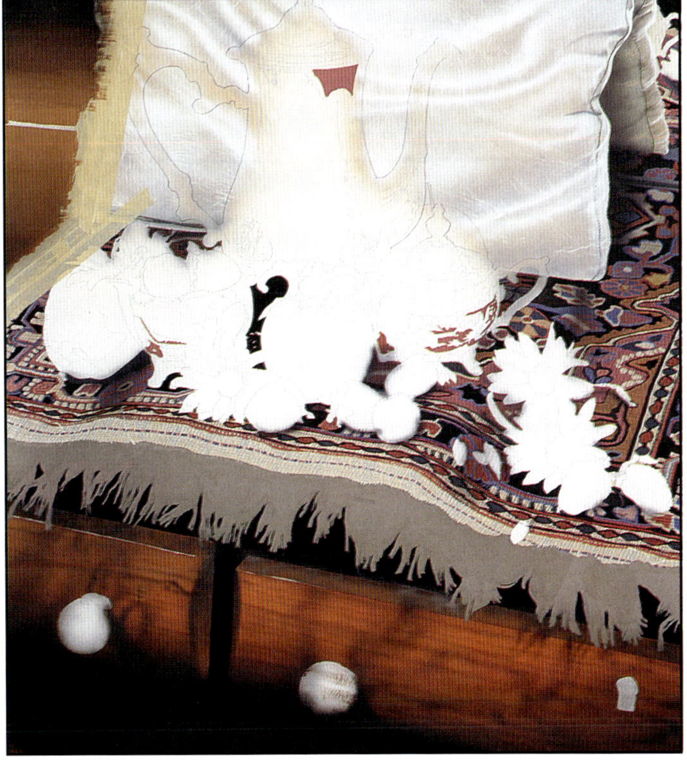

Step 4: Paint the fringe of the rug with a dark mixture of burnt umber, cobalt blue, and Naples yellow. The underpainting is much darker than the actual fringe, which helps create an illusion of shadow.

Step 5: Apply a lighter layer of fringe over the underpainting with Naples yellow and burnt umber. Notice that portions of the darker fringe underneath show through. Paint the drawer knobs, and then reestablish highlights on the drawers.

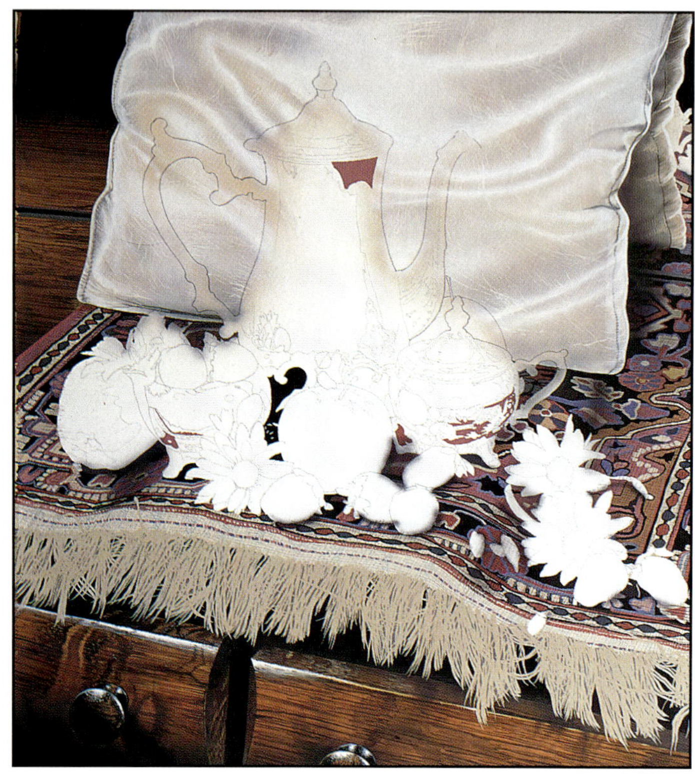

Step 6: Complete the highlights on the fringe. Then paint the basic colors of the strawberries and the top of the teapot. Paint the spout with pure ivory black. Then finish the tiny knob on the lid of the teapot.

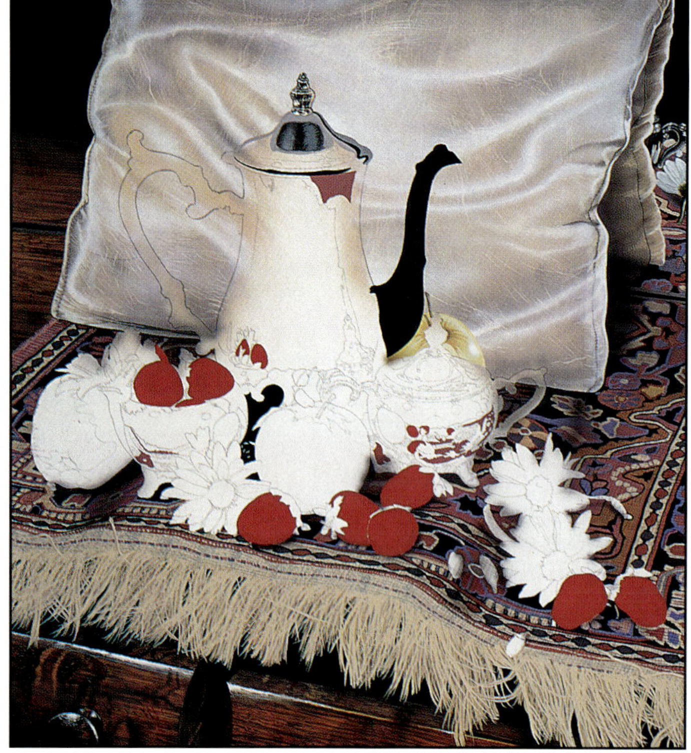

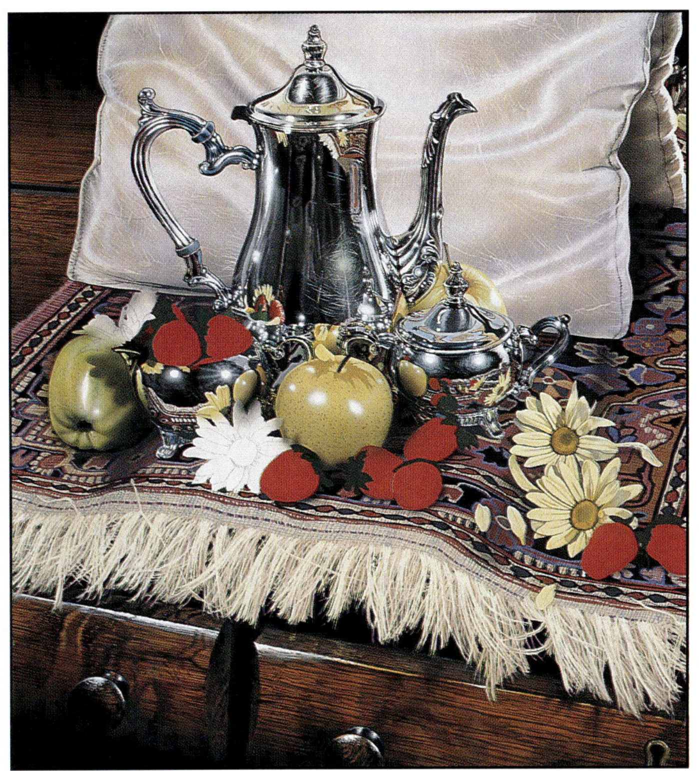

Step 7: Complete all the silver and the three apples. Then paint the flowers. Paint the strawberries last. Silver is easiest to paint by making the entire underpainting black and then carefully observing all the reflections around it. Silver takes on all the colors and shapes around it; it usually distorts the shapes.

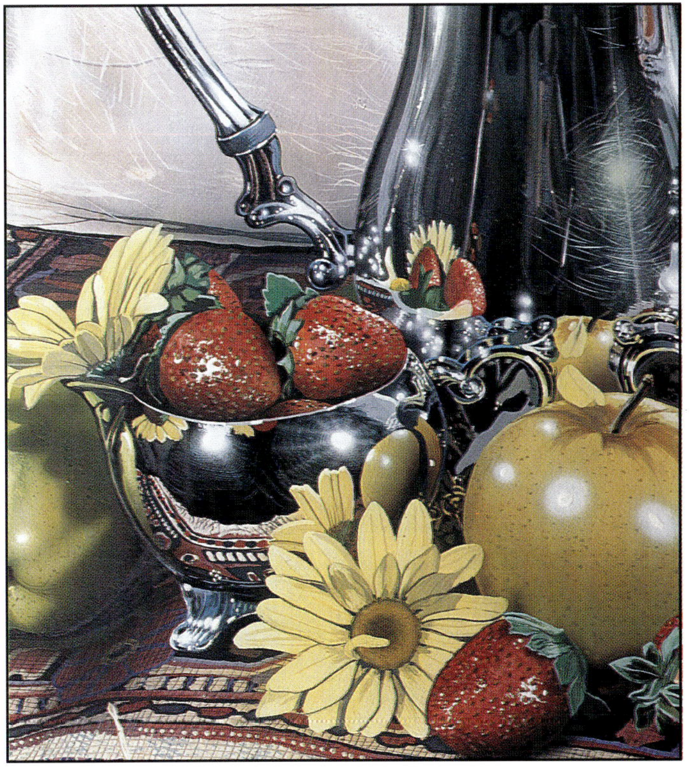

Detail. This close-up of the creamer and surrounding objects demonstrate the precision that gouache can achieve. Notice that the reflections in the creamer are of the surrounding objects. The opacity of gouache makes it a wonderful medium for building layers of light over dark throughout the painting. Additionally, a lot can be accomplished in an hour of painting because it dries so quickly.

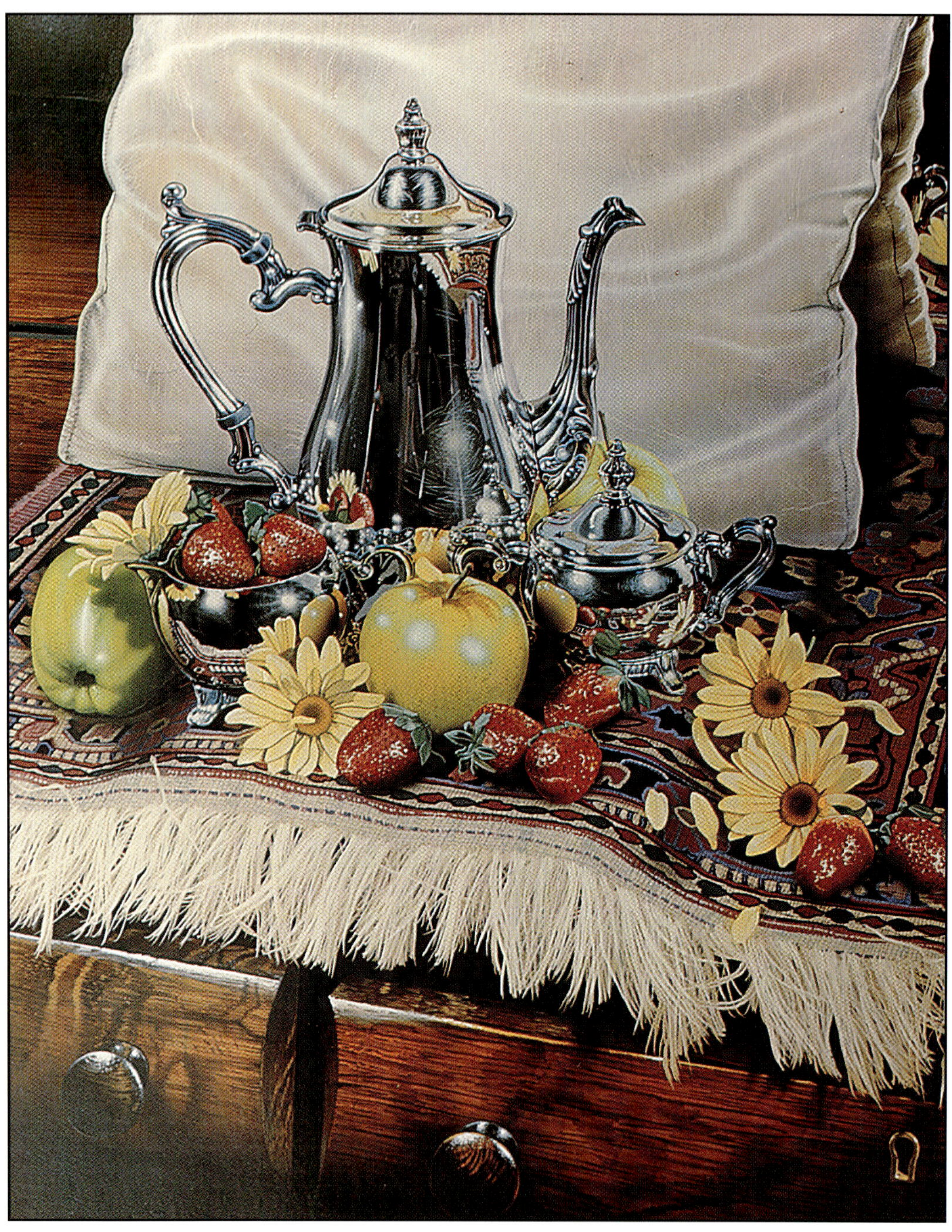

Still Life with Satin Pillow **(32" x 40") gouache on illustration board, private collection**

Finished Painting. The strawberries are the very last item to be completed. They are underpainted in red and shaded slightly with black watercolor. Then the seeds are painted—and highlighted with pure titanium white in the proper areas. Titanium white is a good, permanent hue when used in its pure state but should never be used as a mixing white if you are concerned about permanence.

Making a Stencil

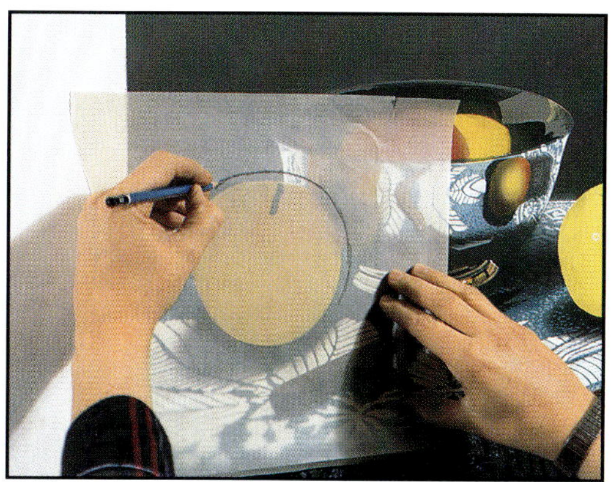

Step 1: You can make stencils with tracing paper, newsprint, and drafting tape. This method is easy and inexpensive; plus, there is less tacky area to stick to the painting. Place a piece of tracing paper over each object to be airbrushed and then trace with an HB pencil at a slightly larger size.

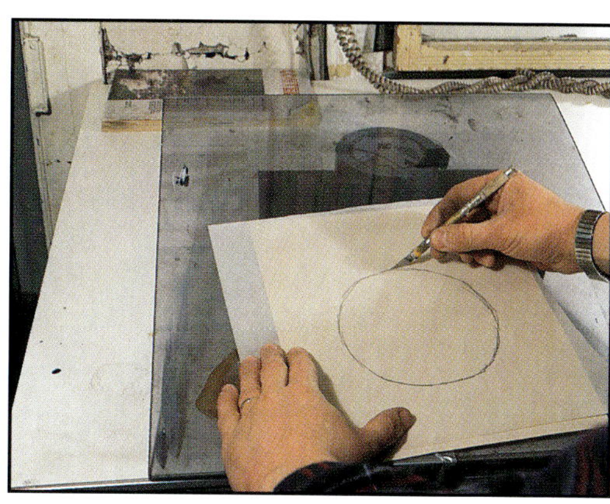

Step 2: Place the tracing paper over a piece of newsprint and cut out the shapes with a single-edge blade or art knife. Use a piece of heavy glass as a cutting board to ensure a precise cut.

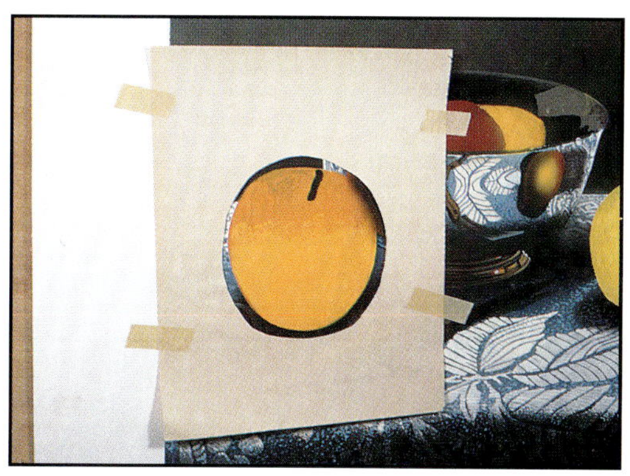

Step 3: Throw out the tracing paper and tape the newsprint stencil over the object. Note: Use drafting tape rather than masking tape to ensure that the paint will not lift when the stencil is removed.

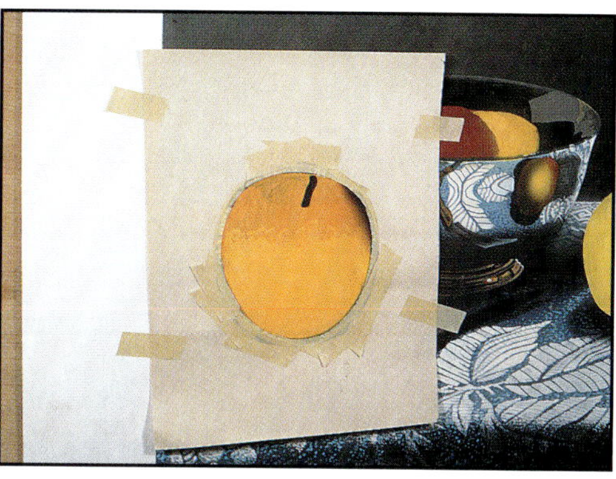

Step 4: Use 1/4" drafting tape to cover the inside edge of the stencil (around the object). The 1/4" tape bends well around curves, protects exposed objects from overspray, and affixes the stencil to the surface of the painting. After airbrushing, allow the paint to dry and then carefully remove the tape to detach the stencil.

Demonstration: *Still Life with Blue Cloth*

Step 1: Sketch the drawing with an HB pencil on hot-pressed illustration board, concentrating on the large, basic shapes. The details will be transferred from the drawing once the painting is begun.

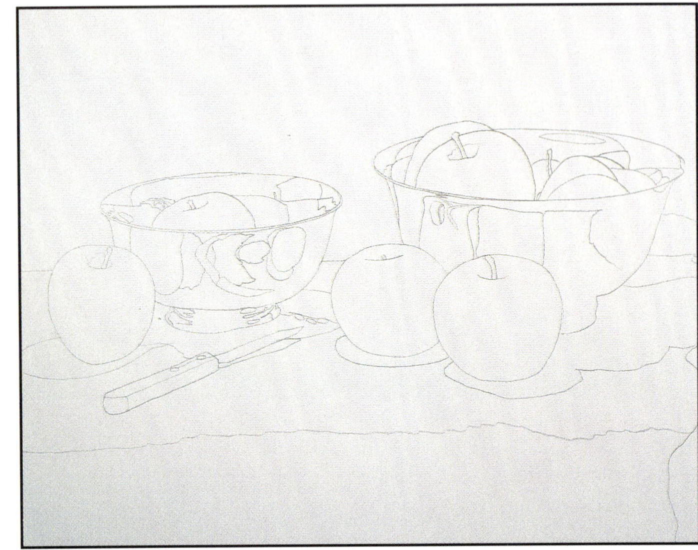

Step 2: Paint the background with an airbrush and black, burnt umber, Naples yellow, alizarin crimson, and viridian gouache. Paint the foreground with a brush, using cerulean blue, cobalt blue, ivory black, and zinc white.

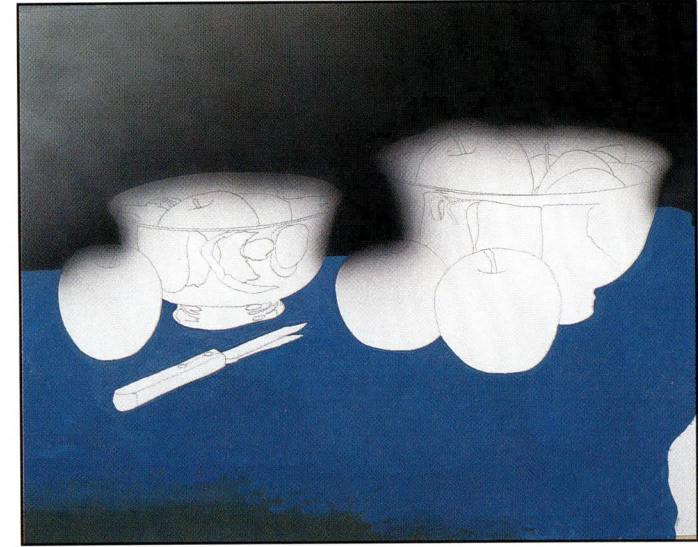

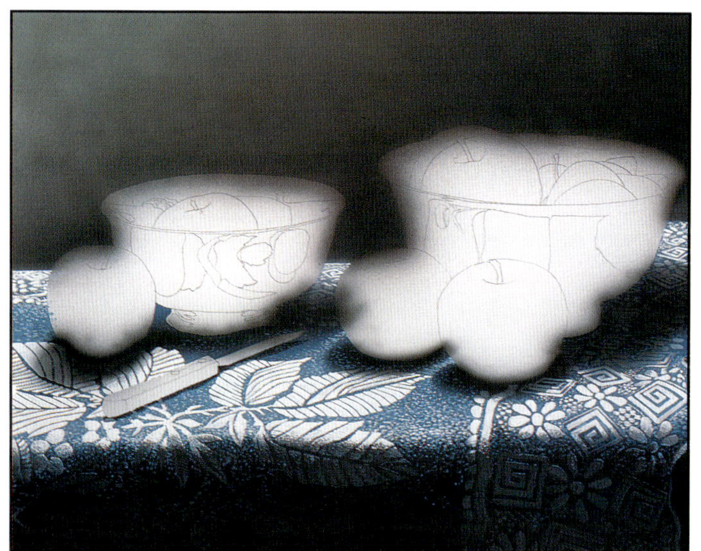

Step 3: After establishing the cloth pattern, use transparent black watercolor to create shadows on the overhanging cloth. Again, the airbrush is an excellent tool for applying watercolor glazes over gouache.

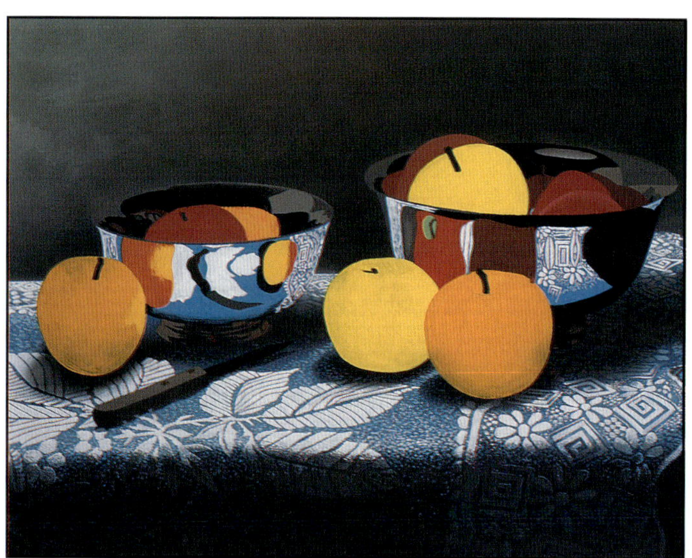

Step 4: Apply a gouache underpainting. Paint most of the fruit lighter than the true local color, but make the reflections of the fruit on the silver darker. Paint the apples from light to dark; the silver from dark to light. The airbrush makes painting apples easy; gouache can be sprayed on in smooth gradations—just like the skin of an apple.

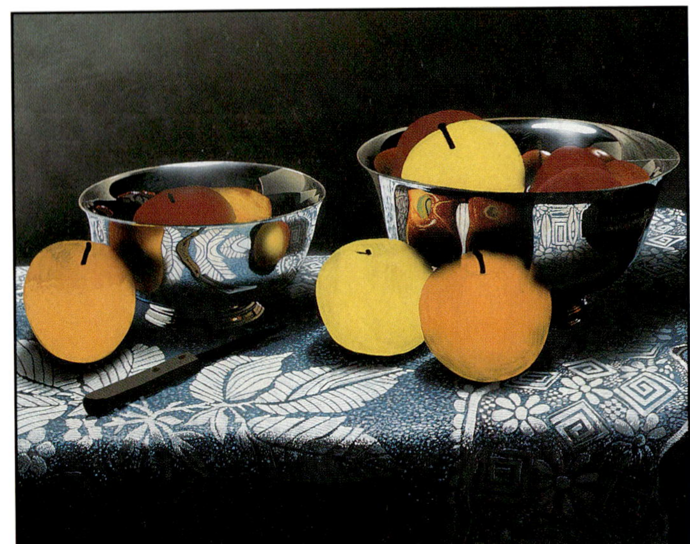

Step 5: Painting silver means painting the reflections of the colors around it. Look for large masses of color in the reflections first, and then paint the small details last. Notice that the cloth, background, fruit, and floodlights are reflected in the silver—all somewhat distorted.

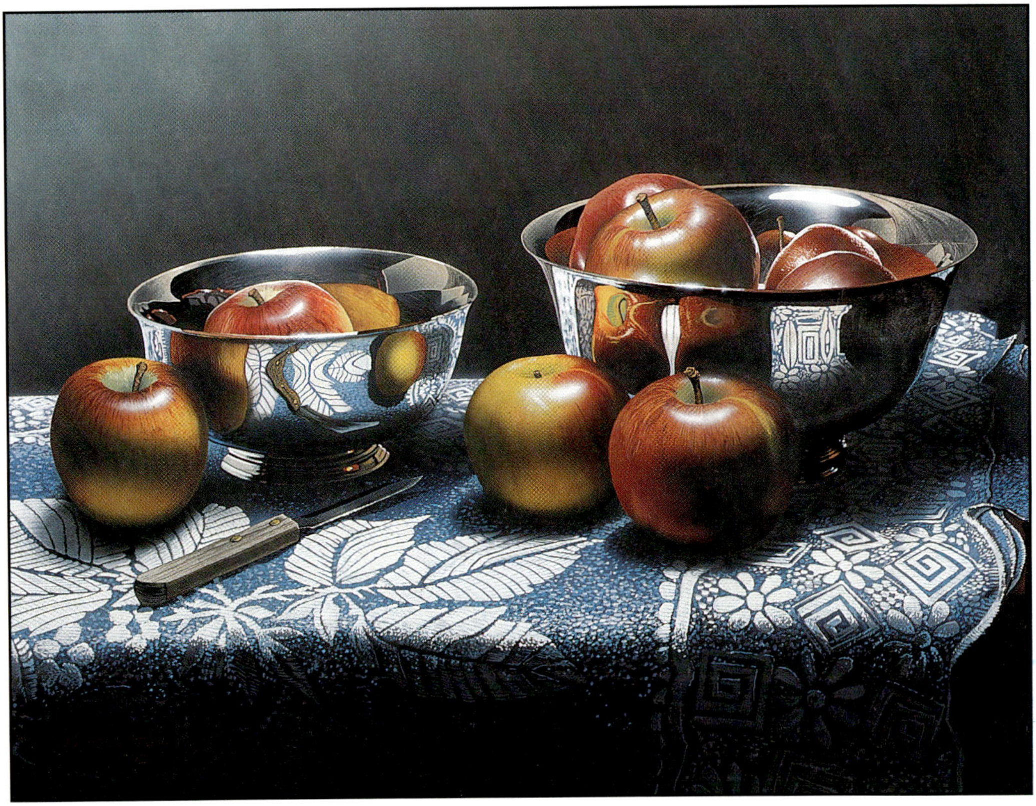

Still Life with Blue Cloth **(24" x 34") gouache on illustration board, collection of Karen Tennant**

Step 6: Complete the painting by finishing the apples and knife. First, airbrush highlights on the apples with titanium white, and then finish off with a small dab of white and a #00 brush. The highlights create a shimmer of intense light on the apples.

Demonstration: *Still Life with Heirlooms*

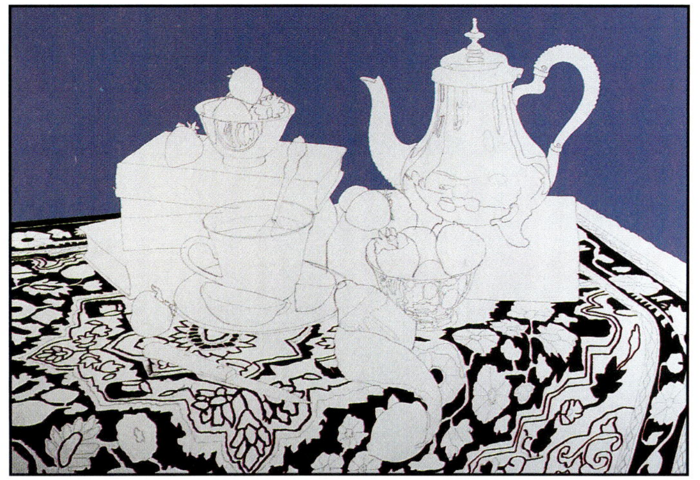

Step 1: Draw the layout for the still life with an HB pencil on hot-pressed illustration board. The HB pencil makes a dark line and maintains a fine point for detailed drawing. Apply the background with a medium-sized watercolor brush and a combination of cerulean blue, cobalt blue, alizarin crimson, and zinc white. Paint in the black patterns on the rug with ivory black.

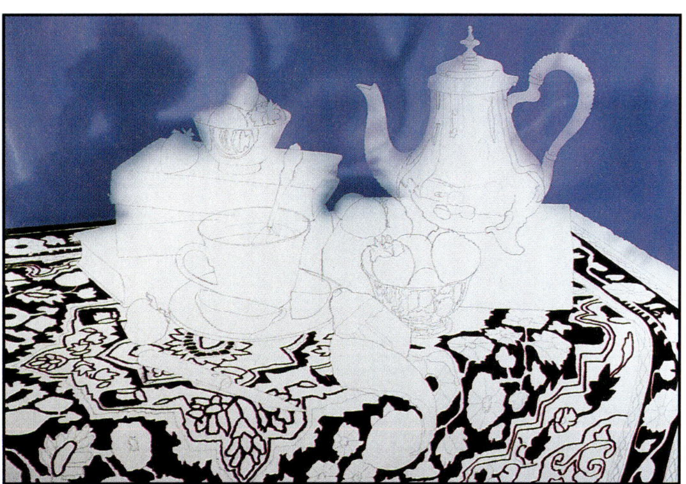

Step 2: Airbrush the darker cast shadows of the background with a transparent watercolor mix of ultramarine blue and ivory black. The transparent watercolor ensures that the blue background can still be seen through the paint film, thus creating a more believable image. Airbrush highlights with a light blue mix of background color and zinc white.

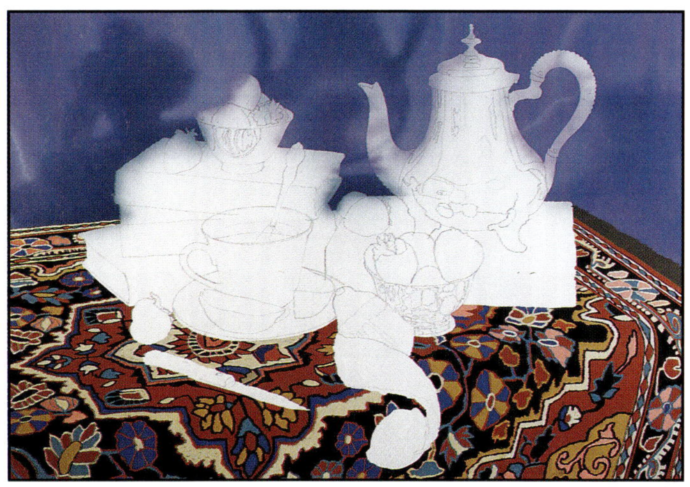

Step 3: Use colors darker than the local colors to underpaint the Persian rug (they will be lightened during the painting process). This is the rule rather the exception. It is rare that an object is painted lighter than needed.

Step 4: Airbrush the shadow on the top of the rug. Then lighten the local colors on the front part of the rug in direct light. To create an interesting pattern and texture, apply hundreds of dots or stipples of lighter color over the darker colors on the rug.

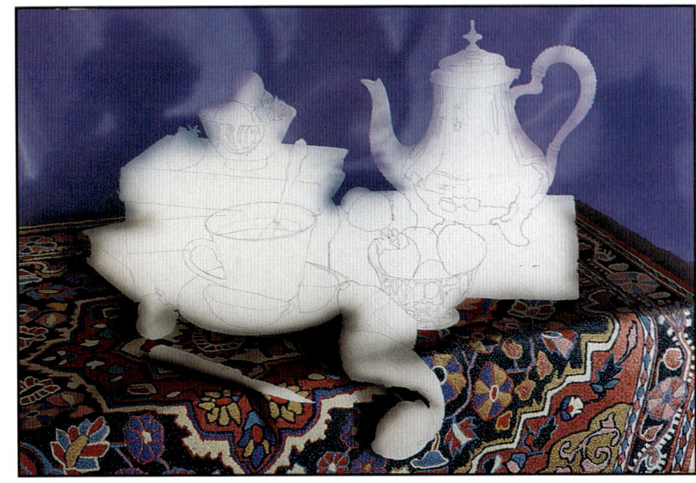

Step 5: Remember, a still life is painted in this order: background, foreground, and then the objects in the foreground. In this example, the books are the next closest objects. The red book is a combination of alizarin crimson, cadmium red, and ivory black. The brown books are burnt umber, ivory black, and zinc white.

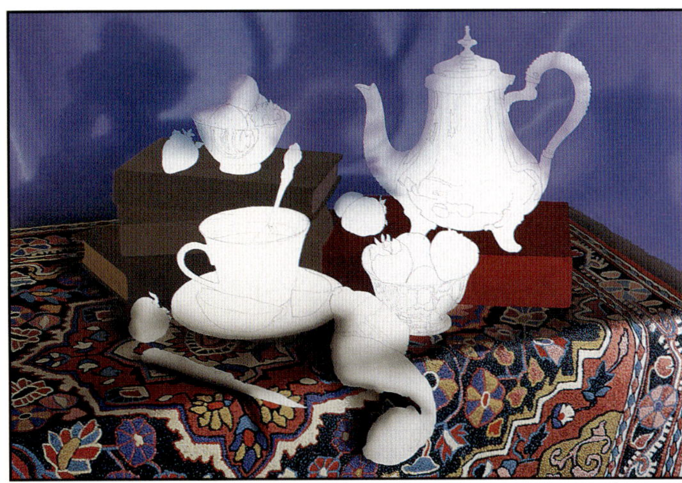

Step 6: Paint the books with details on their spines, as well as textures, highlights, and shadows. Apply the shadows transparently with the airbrush, using straight ivory black watercolor in the proper areas.

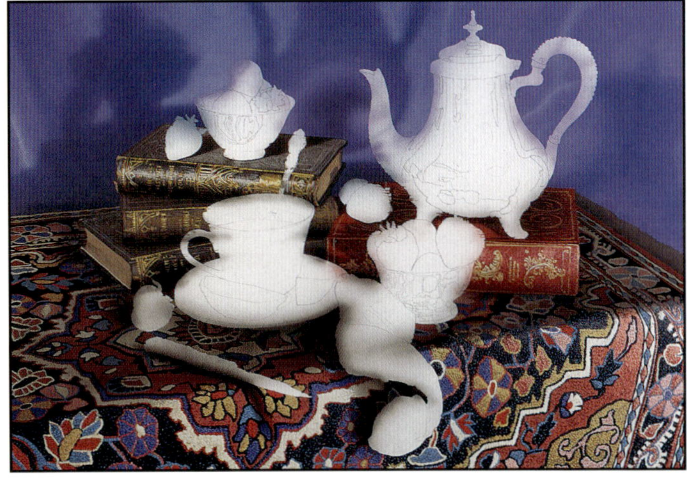

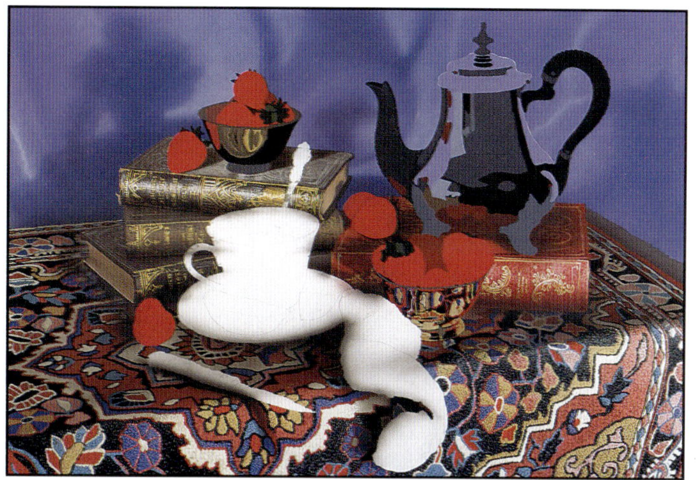

Step 7: Now paint the silver objects—the teapot and two bowls. Then underpaint the strawberries. Remember to work from dark to light on all these objects.

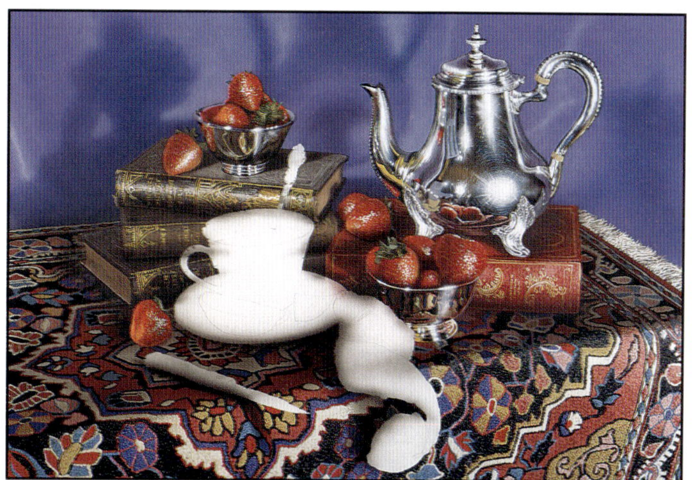

Step 8: After bringing in some lighter reds, shade the strawberries with black watercolor using the airbrush. Then highlight with straight titanium white gouache. Paint the silver to a lighter key, and then shade with the airbrush. As the final touch, apply the highlights—first with the airbrush and then with a brush.

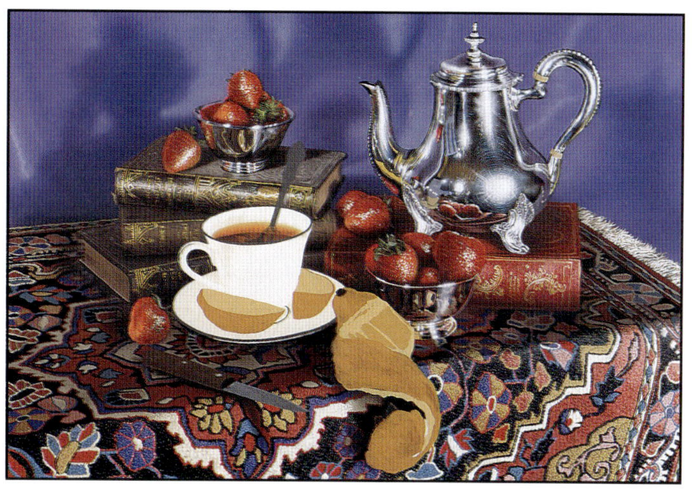

Step 9: Underpaint the teacup and saucer, lemon wedges, and peel darker than they will remain. Note: Most of the objects in this setup are painted from dark to light. The only exceptions are the cup and saucer, which are painted from light to dark.

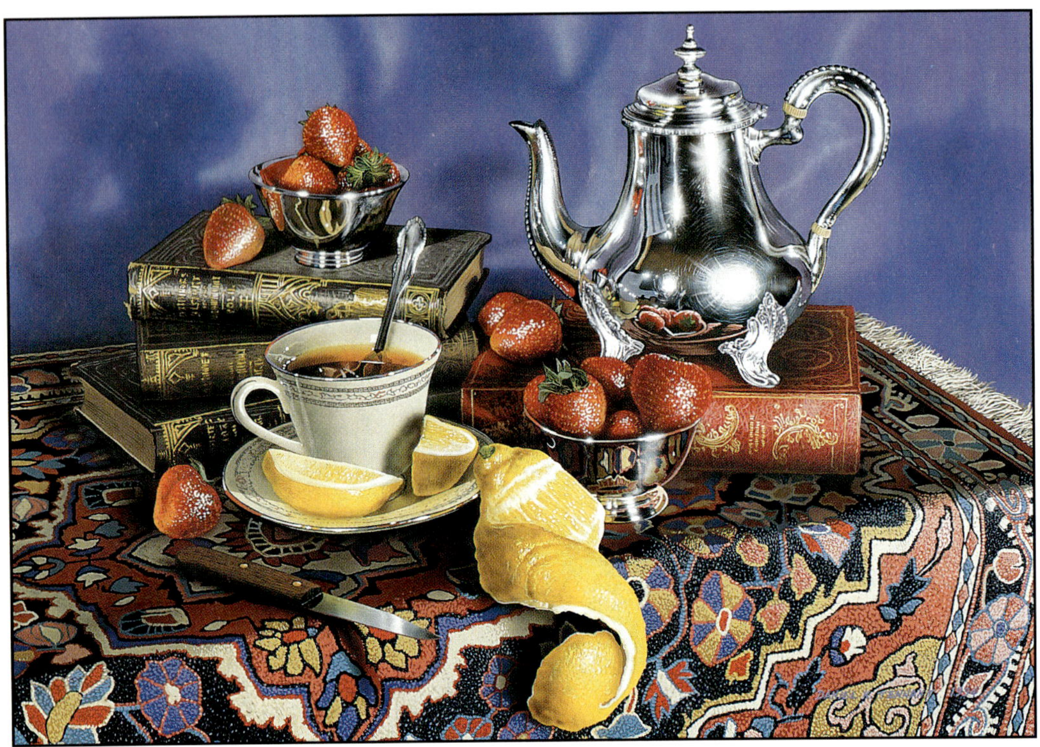

***Still Life with Heirlooms* (24" x 36") gouache on illustration board, collection of David and Judy Mahony**

Step 10: Paint the lemons with yellow ochre, cadmium yellow, and lemon yellow. Then spray medium yellow watercolor over them to intensify the yellows. Lightly spray the shadows on the lemons with ivory black and burnt umber watercolor. Add finishing touches to the spoon and knife. Reestablish all the white highlights to ensure they are at their brightest.

Demonstration: *Winter Sunset*

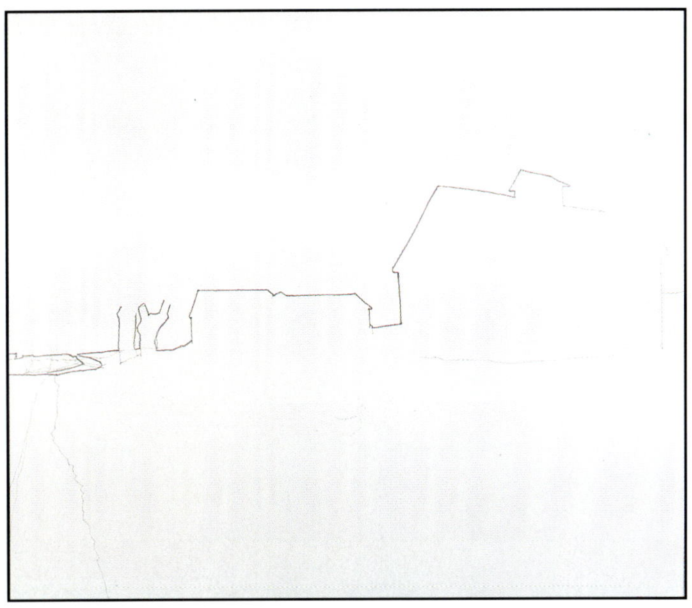

Step 1: Establish the drawing with an HB pencil on illustration board. There is no need for much detail work in the trees because this area will be covered with paint. After the sky is painted, reestablish the background trees and detail by using the tracing paper technique. (See page 10.)

Step 2: Paint the sky with a large, soft-haired flat watercolor brush and a mix of cerulean blue, cobalt blue, and zinc white. Lightly airbrush the yellow clouds over the blue sky with zinc white and cerulean blue mixed with Naples yellow. Try to create light, fluffy clouds; they should not appear solid.

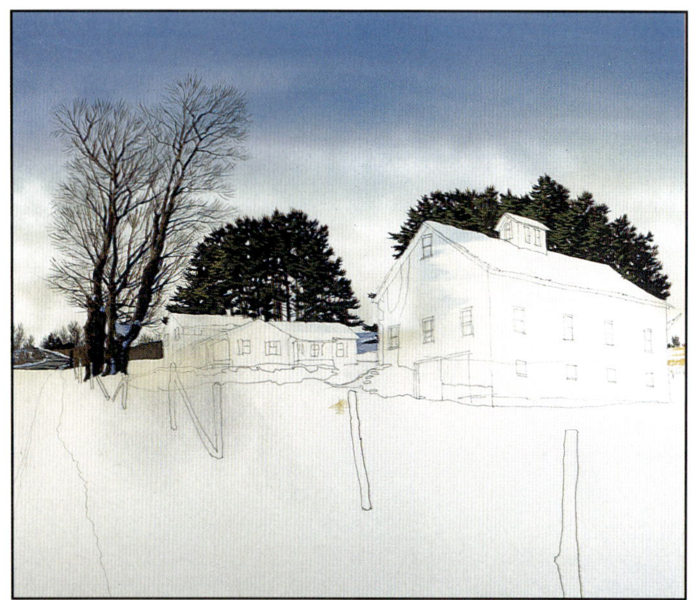

Step 3: When the sky is complete, paint the background. Paint the large pine trees, the distant trees along the horizon, and the receding road with shadows with a small watercolor brush. The pine trees are ivory black and viridian. The background trees are burnt umber and ivory black.

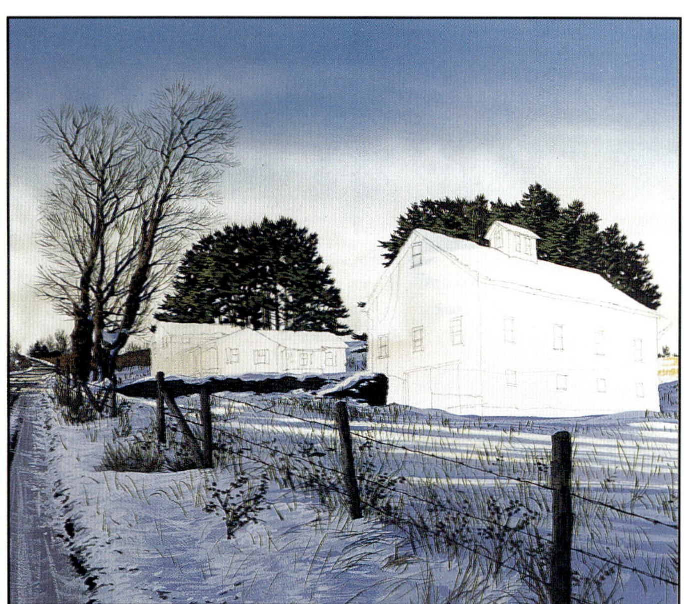

Step 4: Lay in a medium blue of cobalt blue and zinc white, creating the foreground snow. Then add the road and front fence posts. Save the weeds that grow in front of the house for the finishing touches. Paint a landscape in layers to avoid many technical difficulties.

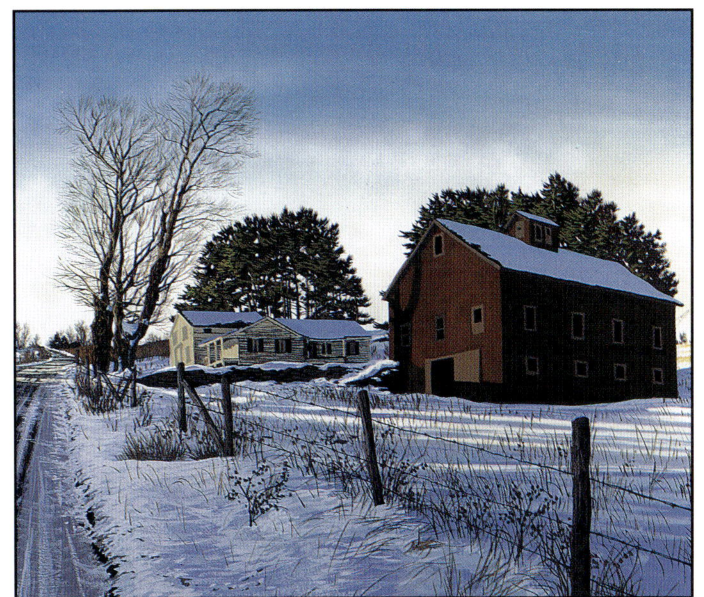

Step 5: Underpaint the buildings. Note that the underpaintings are darker than the final colors on the buildings. When the underpainting is dry, drybrush and spatter the textures on the weathered old barn. The front of the farmhouse is bathed in beautiful evening light, which is raking in direction and warm in its look.

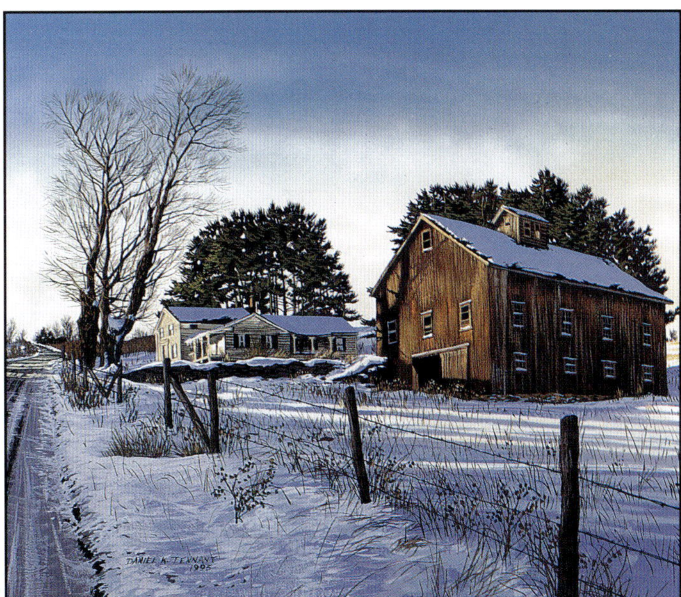

Step 6: To complete the painting, reestablish the highlights, and then add the grasses and minute details throughout the painting. This enhances the final vestiges of the light raking dramatically across the field. Then repaint the weeds in greater numbers.

Winter Sunset **(16" x 20") gouache on illustration board, collection of Fran and Kay Wildenstein**

Gallery

After becoming interested in the various shades of blue that make up snow, I painted this peaceful landscape. The airbrush was necessary to lay in the foggy background in the far woods.

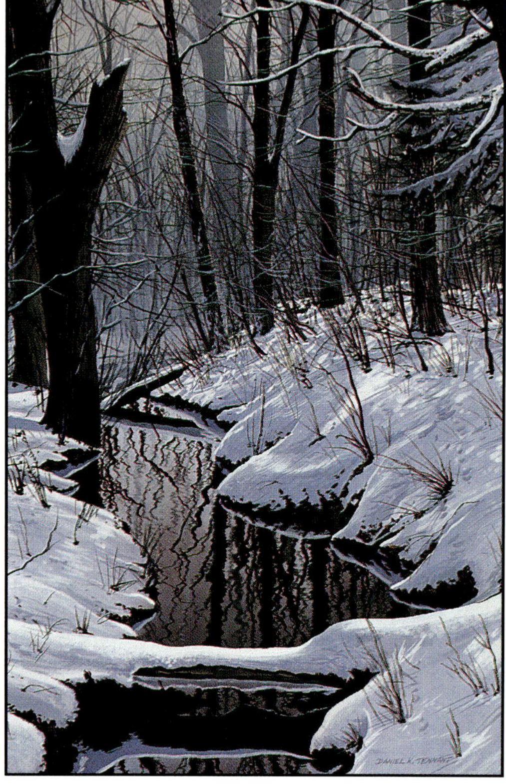

Still Waters **(30" x 22") gouache on gesso panel, private collection**

The large, intricate piece below was painted to explore the variety of textures in an old antique shop. The shadows on the wallpaper were done with airbrush as were the gradated shadows on the crocks.

Crocks on a Quilt **(40" x 60") gouache on museum board, courtesy of Gallery Henoch, New York, NY**

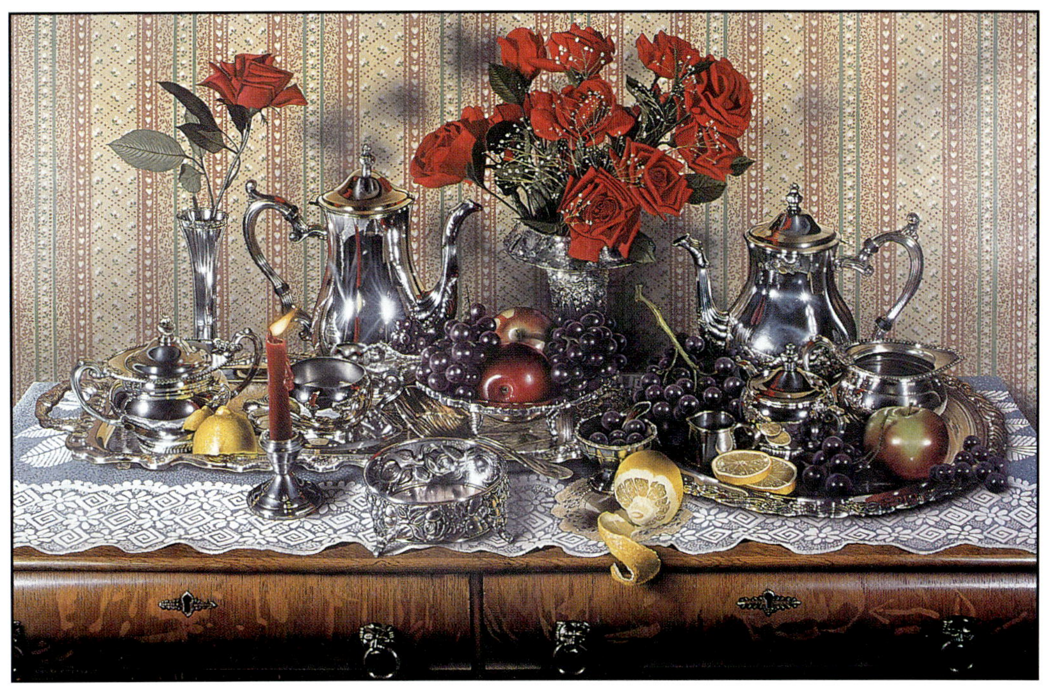

Still Life with Satin Roses **(40" x 60") gouache on museum board, private collection**

A friend of mine has a magnificent collection of silver objects. We put all of them together in this explosion of sparkle and reflections.

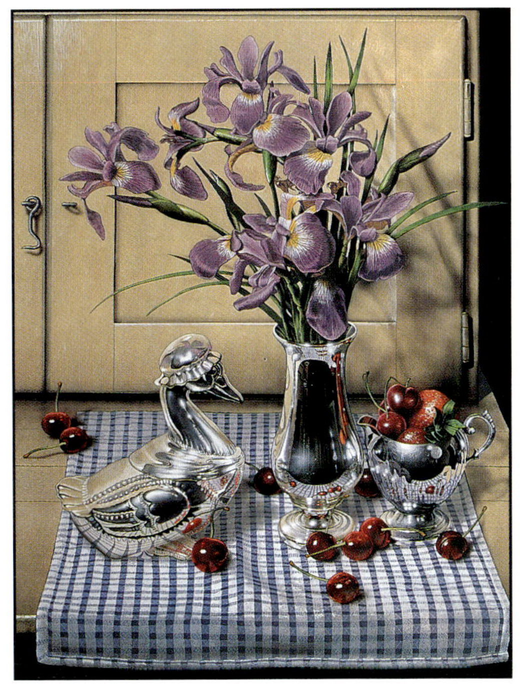

The intriguing aspect of this painting was the way the three different pieces of silver reflected the same objects.

Still Life with Cherries **(32" x 26") gouache on illustration board, private collection**

The central idea was to paint a black-and-white barn surrounded by black-and-white cows. The airbrush was used to create the blowing winds as well as the subtle, stormy sky.

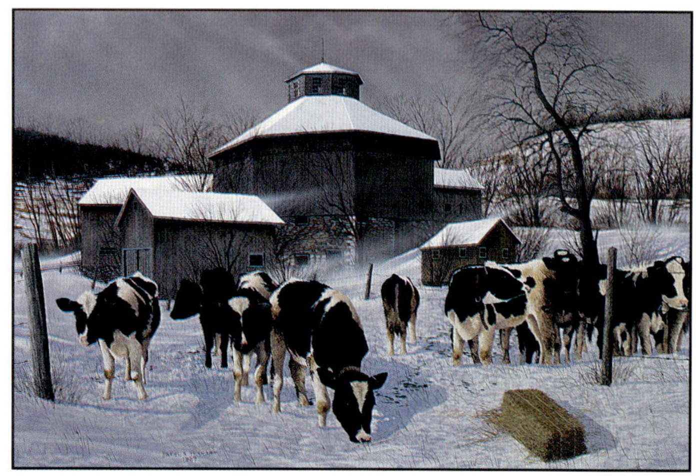

December Winds **(30" x 40") gouache on illustration board, collection of Dr. Gary D. Tennant**

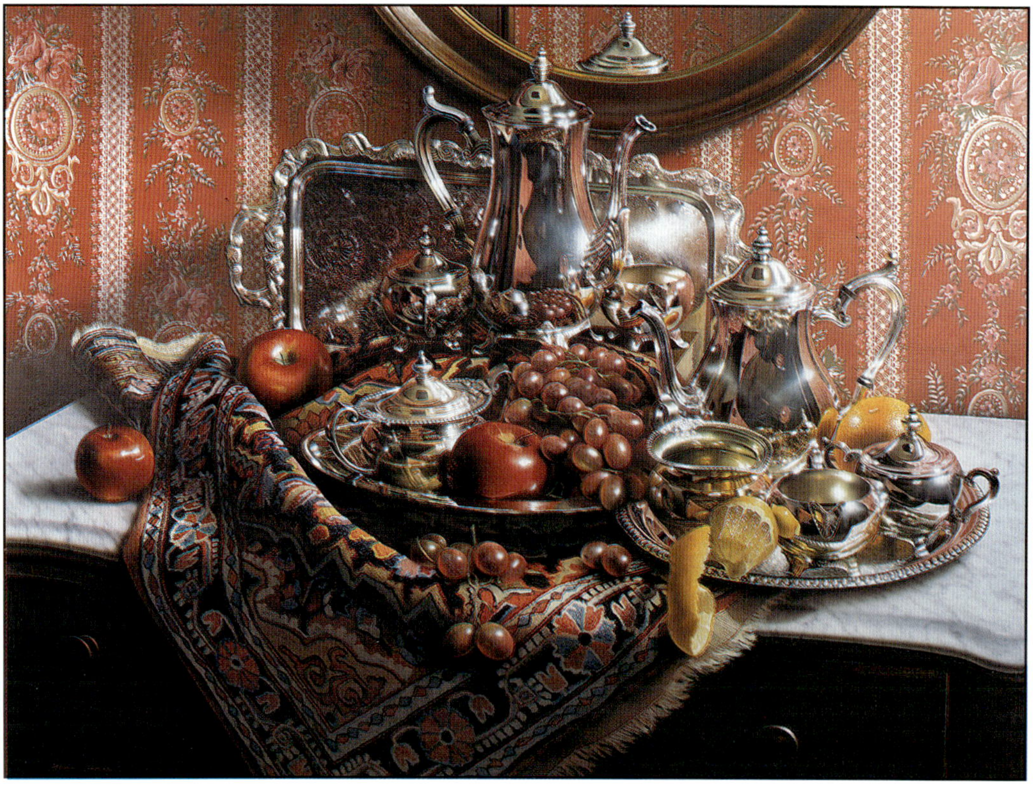

Still Life with Marble-Topped Table **(40" x 50") gouache on museum board, private collection**

In this still life, I was interested in how the various textures—fruit, silver, glass, wood, wallpaper, tapestry—worked together. The biggest challenge was capturing the way the silver picked up the wonderful textures and reflections of light.

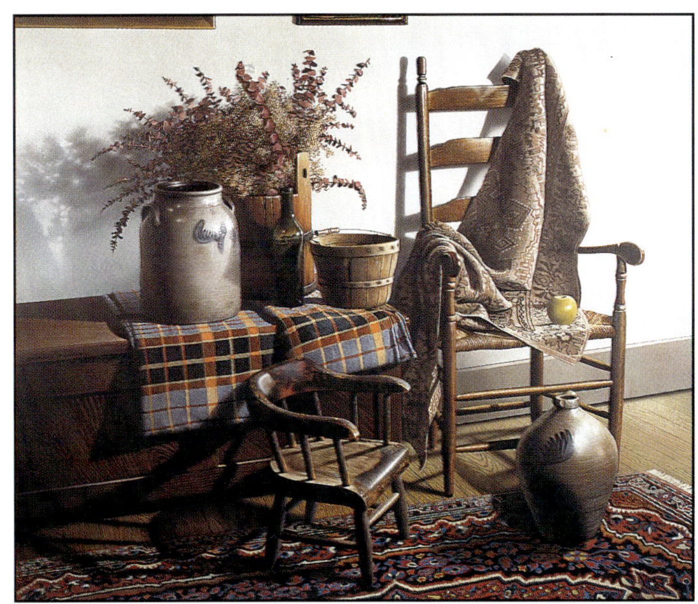

Having found this setup as is—except for a few changes—it was indeed a pleasant find! The soft gradations of the background were achieved by the gentle spray of the airbrush. Gouache is superb for the most intricate detail work. Portions of this painting were achieved by using artist-grade colored pencils. Gouache can also be used very effectively with pastel as well.

A Pleasant Find **(40" x 50") gouache on museum board, courtesy of Gallery Henoch, New York, NY, and Moriah Publishing, Beachwood, OH**

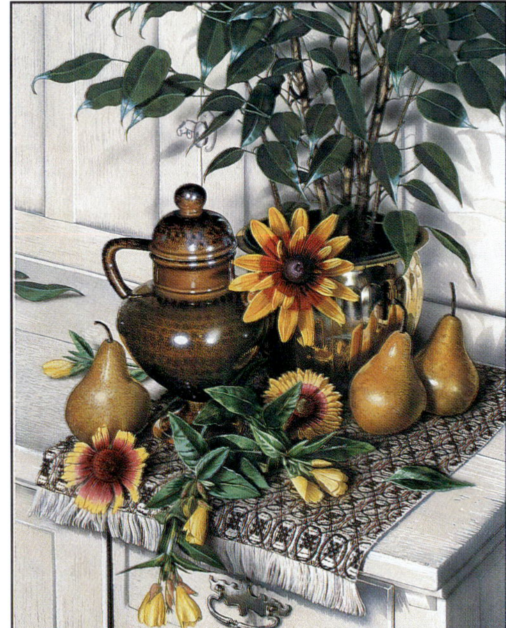

Still Life with Sundrops **(24" x 34") gouache on illustration board, courtesy of Gallery Henoch, New York, NY**

The main interest here is the brass plant holder (a yellow metal). Close observation of lighting, shadows, and textures helps to give a feeling of reality to the piece.

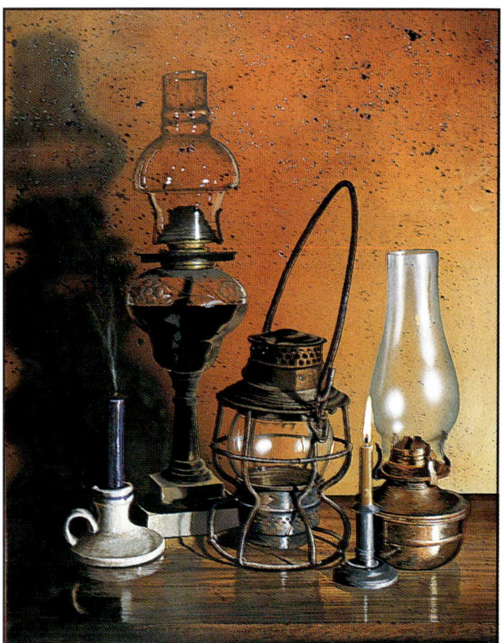

Still Life with Five Lanterns **(30" x 40") gouache on illustration board, private collection**

Airbrushing the shadow provided more contrast with the lanterns. The airbrush extends the capabilities of gouache.

Final Thoughts

I would like to offer some parting advice. Keep a notebook of tips, ideas, and quotes that speak to you as an artist. Refer to it for encouragement, help, and inspiration. Establish a good working library of reference books on materials, techniques, and whatever you like to paint. Visit art shows and talk to other artists for advice and help. Subscribe to good art magazines that fit your needs. Always buy the best materials—especially brushes. Don't get discouraged. Give yourself room to grow as an artist—you will.

Listen to good music when you paint. Make prints and slides of all your work and keep them on file so you can gauge your improvement. Take time off to do other things, then your art will be better.

I hope the instructions throughout this book will help you achieve a higher level of painting skills. A lifetime of technique and thought has gone into this book. I wish you all the very best as you implement the many ideas found in this book.

I would like to acknowledge the following people: Karen, my wife, who is my best critic and strongest supporter; my children—Christopher, Andrew, Bethany, and Megan—my four masterpieces; Rob Howard, who provided excellent information about gouache; Dan Harrington and Elisabeth Stuart for modeling; Steve Doherty, a great encourager; the memory of Merrill A. Bailey, an artist and teacher with humility; Wendall Upchurch, a walking encyclopedia of technical information about paints; Gallery Henoch for supplying excellent visuals; George H. Shechtman, the best art dealer any artist could ever have; the Rev. L.F. Caruana, friend, supporter, and pastor; and my Creator, who gave the gift of art and who is the greatest artist of all.

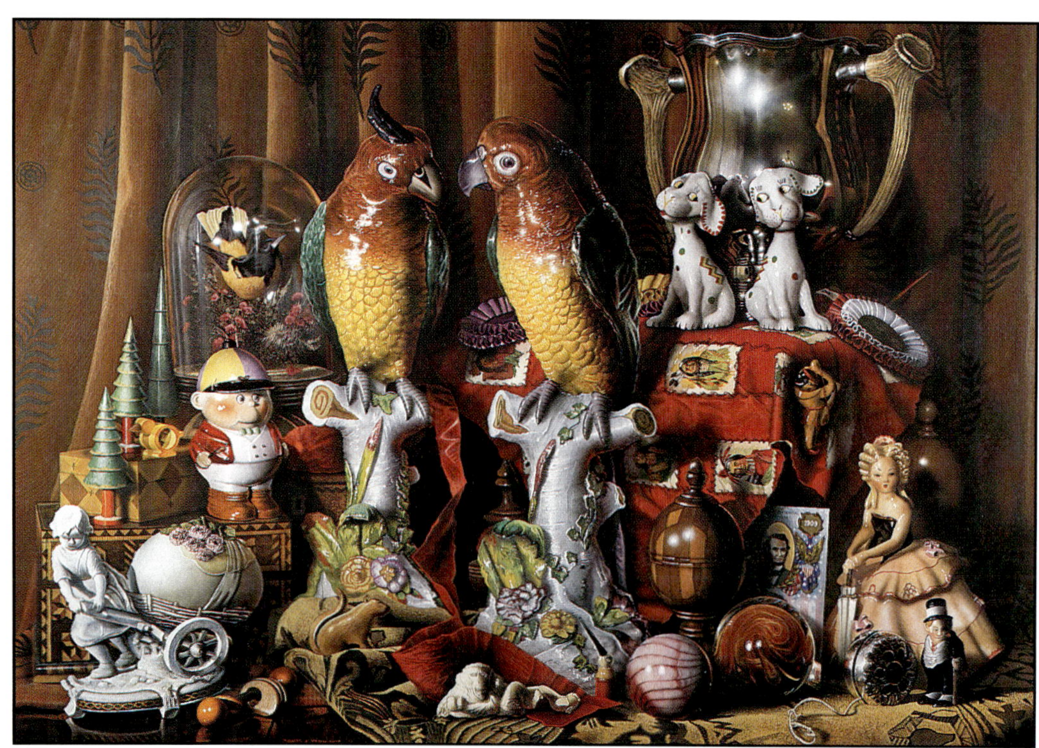

***Fancier's Fantasy* (40" x 60") gouache on museum board, private collection**